Getting ... the game

CUSTOMER EXPERIENCE IS THE BRAND

Alex Allwood

For my book-loving husband

Customer Experience is the Brand

First published in Australia in 2015 by
Holla Advertising (Australia) Pty Limited
T/A The Holla Agency (Australia)
Suite 3, 65-67 Foveaux Street
Surry Hills, NSW, 2010

Visit our website: thehollaagency.com.au

ISBN: 978-0-9943433-8-3

A catalogue entry is available for this book from
the National Library of Australia

Cover design by The Holla Agency
Internal design and book production by Michael Hanrahan Publishing
Printed in Australia by McPherson's Printing

Contents

Introduction   1

PART ONE: THE EXPERIENCE ECONOMY

01   Hello Customer Experience   7

02   The Experience Evolution   13

03   Empowered Consumerism   19

04   Generation Next   23

05   Always On   27

06   The Business Case   31

PART TWO: THE 7 PILLARS OF CUSTOMER EXPERIENCE

07   Where to Begin   39

08   Pillar One: Brand Purpose   47

09   Pillar Two: Organisational Alignment   57

10   Pillar Three: Customer Journey   63

11   Pillar Four: Keeping the Promise   73

12   Pillar Five: Technology   81

13   Pillar Six: Co-creation   89

14   Pillar Seven: Experience Management   97

PART THREE: MARKETING THE EXPERIENCE

15 Mobile First 109

16 Making it Personal 117

17 Brands as Publishers 125

18 When Art Meets Science 131

19 Paid Media 135

20 Sharing the Buzz 147

21 Customer Surprise and Delight 153

22 Ready, Aim, Fire 157

About the author 161

Bibliography 163

Introduction

This book has been written for marketing and business leaders who value marketing and champion the customer. Those leaders who want to be change-makers in their industry, who are interested in not just keeping up or keeping current but want to be ahead of the curve. Leaders who have become accustomed to change and are comfortable with its relentless pace and who understand how technology and data can enable the transformation of their organisation's marketing.

Customers are now in the driver's seat. Everything is at their fingertips. They are global and super-connected, with expectations that their brand interactions will be personalised, contextual and device relevant. For this reason, organisations will need to refocus on their customer, developing an organisation-wide commitment to brand/customer experiences where customer needs are consistently met, brand promises are kept, and every touchpoint in the customer journey delivers a positive experience.

Customer experience is the next stage in the evolution of the brand. For brand leaders with step-change on their agenda and an appetite for transforming customer relationships, the book introduces the principles of customer experience, helping to galvanise customer value creation, deliver competitive advantage, strengthen brand preference and create sustained growth.

Customer Experience is the Brand is an introduction to customer experience strategy using 'The 7 Pillars of Customer Experience' as the foundation for building strong connections throughout the business to create a customer-first culture that fosters satisfaction and advocacy. The book uses research, expert comment, thought leadership and my own experience to synthesise current thinking on customer experience. Brand leadership case studies are referenced to highlight best practice and give readers additional insight into how great customer experiences can transform brands.

Now is the time when 'customer experience is the brand', where brand leaders will need to understand their brand's reason for being – its purpose – create organisational alignment around a customer-first culture, consistently deliver and keep the brand promise, find customer truths and create simple, feel-good experiences that people want to talk about and share with their friends and social networks.

At stake for businesses are branded moments that fail to satisfy customer needs, leaving customers ambivalent and open to amplifying their disappointment publicly. With this in mind, marketers are perfectly placed to be the custodians of their organisation's customer experiences;

bringing together their expertise and leadership in the areas of brand, customer, data, technology, innovation, marketing and digital design to positively influence internal alignment around the customer relationship with the brand.

The balance of power for marketers is shifting; increasingly they are being asked for strategic input to influence their business's future direction through customer value creation. To be the custodians of the experience agenda and have their strategic contribution to business growth valued, marketers will need to rapidly reshape their portfolios and redefine their roles, building customer-centric brands to meet changing customer demands.

The experience economy is here, our customers are living it now, and now is the time for brands to catch up – welcome to *Customer Experience is the Brand*.

Part One

THE EXPERIENCE ECONOMY

01

Hello Customer Experience

This is the digital era, a time when the modern marketer has been forced to evolve from *communications expert* to *custodian of customer experience*. This is a time when innovation is disrupting the marketing status quo, marketing and technology are intertwined, and the pace of change continues to accelerate; when the customer journey starts with a click; and when the 'moment-of-truth' – a customer making a decision to buy or not to buy – is based on what they *experience*.

Our responses, opinions, attitudes and behaviours are all directly related to the situations and events we have experienced. What people experience is what they remember, and the more emotional the experience the deeper the memory. Because of this, people form brand perceptions through the quality of experience they have. Put simply, customer experience is the brand perception customers hold resulting from *every* digital and physical interaction – it's how customers feel about the brand, and these perceptions are formed through every interaction.

When customers have a positive experience it impacts their purchasing decisions and determines what's talked about with their friends and peers. Great brand experiences are stories that customers want to talk about and share with their social networks. These experiences are relevant, simple, feel-good moments at every customer/brand interaction, whether it be viewing an ad, searching and researching, using a mobile app, shopping in-store, buying online or calling customer service.

That was then

Yesterday's marketing was the art of winning customers through advertising, promotions and public relations in a time when the brand message was broadcast from the business to the audience. With the advent of the smartphone and social media, yesterday's marketing model has become just that: a model that's not as relevant in the experience economy any more. Experiences therefore need to be managed at each and every touchpoint and marketers need to ensure that these moments deliver the brand promise in a compelling and relevant way across digital and physical channels. Customer experiences have quickly become the new focus for organisations in the digital era.

This is now

What has rapidly become today's marketing is more than a one-way communication. Customer experience translates into developing an ongoing relationship at every touchpoint between a brand and the customer, with greater importance attached to what is being said about the experience online. And therein lies the challenge for the modern marketer, because what the customer experiences dictates what people are saying about the brand to their friends in real-world conversations, in social media, in online reviews and in discussion forums.

The influence of word-of-mouth

Customers are making themselves heard as never before, and brands are now being defined by what the customer experiences. Thanks to online search and social media, today's customers are able to easily find, research, purchase, review and share their brand experiences. For considered purchases the customer's first touchpoint in brand discovery will most likely be online, searching for the product or service, reading reviews or using their social networks for information. Word-of-mouth has also become more influential in brand decision-making. People now feel completely at ease in sharing their opinions online with their friends and their networks, and the instantaneous nature of an online *love or hate* or *good or bad* post by a customer means their experience can go viral and be read by thousands of people in a matter of minutes; the problem for brands is that bad news always seems to travel faster!

Custodian of the customer

The next challenge for marketers is to transition from their traditional portfolio of brand communications expert to custodian of the entire customer experience: from brand awareness through to customer service interaction. Given marketers' understanding of customer needs, brand promise creation and their focus on data and technology, marketers are best placed to redefine the customer experience. On their agenda will be driving business growth through culturally aligning the organisation around the customer, uniting the brand with a powerful purpose, dismantling organisational silos and ensuring brand promises are kept across each touchpoint to deliver a positive end-to-end experience that customers want to talk about.

Recent figures show that revenue growth from a modest improvement in customer experience can yield significant returns, and this has prompted some senior marketers to push for full control of the customer experience. Deloitte's paper on *Bridging The Digital Divide* reports that smart marketers who understand the direct relationship between customer experience and business growth are setting about collaborating with other departments within their organisations to streamline and automate internal systems and processes.[1] By rethinking the customer/brand ecosystem, smart marketers will bring together sales and marketing,

---

1   'Bridging The Digital Divide, How CMO's Can Rise to Meet 5 Expanding Expectations', Deloitte, 2014

customer service, product development and operations to evolve the customer experience and create continuous and seamless experiences throughout the purchase journey.

02

The Experience Evolution

Today, people have many more product and service choices through many more channels than ever before. In the late nineties, authors Pine and Gilmore introduced the idea that the experience economy was the new economy post the evolution of the agrarian, industrial and service economies.[2] As services become increasingly commoditised (like goods before them), the next competitive advantage for brands is providing experiences.

Economic stages

Pine and Gilmore identified four distinct economic stages and outlined how each of these has changed over time. In the agrarian economy, commodities were produced from the soil and sold in the open market. In the second stage industrial economy manufactured goods became the predominant economic offering. In the next half century

2   B Joseph Pine II and James H Gilmore, 'Welcome to the Experience
      Economy', *Harvard Business Review*, July–August 1998 Issue

manufactured goods gradually became commoditised and people's buying criteria became more price focused.

The third stage, service economy, evolved from the customisation of goods to deliver economic value in the form of services, and – like the economies before it – the service economy too has gradually become commoditised. Pine and Gilmore maintain that the experience economy, the fourth economic stage, will evolve from the service economy to become the predominant vehicle of economic value. For most businesses the shift will not be easy.

In this fourth stage, the experience economy is set to deliver personalisation of services that are unique, real and created with customer involvement, fitting with their needs at any moment in time. The heart of customer experience is authenticity. Authenticity is knowing what the brand stands for, its purpose, beliefs and truths. Authentic brands have meaning and are committed to delivering what they promise with clear offerings and an appetite to forge emotional connections with their customers.

A customer experience is the interaction between the customer and the brand and is based on an individual's emotions, sensory and behavioural cues, and their personal interpretation, and is defined as the 'perceptions, feelings and thoughts that customers have when they encounter products and brands'. Experiences 'may be evoked by products, packaging, communications, in store interactions, sales relationships and events...'[3] Designed with

---

3   Hélder Ferreira and Aurora AC Teixeira, '"Welcome to the Experience Economy": Assessing the Influence of Customer Experience Literature Through Bibliometric Analysis', January 2013

deep understanding of customer needs, engaging experiences deliver brand differentiation in today's marketplace.

Customer experiences offer organisations the opportunity to emotionally differentiate their businesses in a highly competitive and commoditised market. In today's experience economy, to leverage the differentiation and competitive advantage that experiences deliver, brands need to shift from simply wrapping an experience around their existing product and service offering to developing experiences that people are willing to pay a premium for. In order to make this shift, businesses need to design and integrate the customer's physical and digital experience to evoke positive emotions throughout the customer purchase journey – in doing so, delivering deep engagement, satisfaction and brand advocacy.

An appetite for more

Coffee – the busy person's favourite morning beverage – embodies the progression of economic value. The humble coffee bean at its core is a commodity; enough beans for a single cup would probably set you back 20¢. Roast, grind, freeze-dry and package it to sell at the supermarket: $1 per cup. For many people, coffee on the go is now part of their morning routine, and this requires the services of a barista at the local cafe to brew a delicious hot coffee in a take-away cup – at $3.50. Take this same service and add flavours such as caramel, cinnamon or vanilla and now we have the experience of speciality coffee, which the

Starbucks customer – for example – can personalise to suit their taste, for a premium $4.00-plus per cup. However, it would seem that our appetite for the flavoured coffee experience is waning, and in the wings is the next generation of customer experience in cafe culture. Recent winner of the Design for Excellence Award for Complete Customer Experience is the Workshop Cafe in San Francisco. The brand successfully pinpointed an on-the-go customer segment whose appetite for coffee and technology has now been satisfied by providing ergonomic working spaces with plenty of power outlets, widescreen monitors, printers, scanners and fast WIFI; all combined with the social cafe experience.

Prior to opening the Workshop Cafe, the startup undertook a customer journey analysis to gain valuable customer insights, 'through time-span observation, contextual inquiry, insight sorting and frame-working, [the brand] built a spectrum of types of users for Workshop and then built out the top physical, experiential, digital, and service design opportunities. [The] big insight about user needs was that time of day was the most important factor in terms of style of work performed. [So the business] built [their] spaces and experiences to accommodate this.'[4]

The customer experience was designed to be iterative and responsive, with the cafe's ecosystem built on 'simple, streamlined, productive and healthy experience.'[5] A mobile app enables customers to reserve seats and order food and

4   Design for Excellence Awards, Customer Experience, Workshop Cafe, 2014
5   Ibid

beverages without having to queue or compete for seating, and includes a community page that allows customers to network. Data collected gives a continual loop of customer feedback and learnings, enabling reorganisation of the cafe's modular furniture design for better seating layouts and adjustment to cafe operations.

The experience is where the economic value lies for the Workshop Cafe; merging physical with digital to deliver a customer experience that encompasses the brand's employees, the physical space, food and technology, to deliver a new type of customer experience, and in doing so disrupting the traditional style of cafe culture. Re-engineering the experience by integrating technology and enabling customers to participate in designing their own personalised experience creates deep and memorable connections to deliver strong competitive advantage, one for which the customer is willing to pay a premium of $2 per hour.

03

Empowered Consumerism

We are experiencing a period in our economic history of abundance and affordability; an era of high-tech platforms, digitisation of products and social networks, renewed importance of community, and value placed on the sustainability of resources. These are the drivers of an economic model that's called *collaborative consumption*, based on shared access to goods and services rather than private ownership. Its popularity is being driven by Millennials (Generation Y), using technology and social media to connect with communities and likeminded individuals who value empowered consumerism.

Peer-to-peer marketplaces

Peer-to-peer (P2P) online marketplaces are redefining how people access today's products and services. From accommodation (Airbnb), car rental (GoGet) and car sharing (GreenCarShare), running errands (Airtasker), skills for hire (oDesk) to trading currency (Bitcoin), the P2P brands are unlocking the traditional marketplace and bringing people and/or businesses together via the internet to deal with each other directly and without the middle man. This is an online marketplace that's shifting passive consumption to highly enabled collaborators, and in the process is delivering greater cost savings and addressing long-held sustainability questions with more efficient use of resources.

Armed with a smartphone and an appetite for change, the marketplace is being reinvented by people who are willing to experience a different way of purchasing and consuming the things they need and want. Collaborative consumption is enabling them to barter, swap and share unutilised or under-utilised resources that are sitting idle, whether this is rooms in people's homes, cars and bikes, or personal skills. Rachel Botsman, author of *What's Mine is Yours*, uses an example of power drill usage: 'That a power drill will be used around 12 to 13 minutes in its entire lifetime is kind of ridiculous, right? Because what you need is the hole, not the drill.'[6]

Value driven

In this new value-driven economy the biggest impact is being felt at present by the taxi, travel and leisure industries. New brands on the block Uber (recently valued at $48.11 billion USD[7]) and Airbnb (valued at $20 billion

---

6   'The Case for Collaborative Consumption', TED, 2010

7   'Is Uber Really Worth $48 Billion', News.com.au, 8 December 2014

USD[8]) are disrupting established brands with their new business models and in both cases changing purchasing behaviour to the detriment of existing businesses. Jeremiah Owyang, the founder of Silicon Valley's Crowd Companies Council, wrote in a recent blog that San Francisco newspaper *SF Chronicle* had reported the taxi industry was suffering a 65% loss in rides and a study by Boston University showed that for every 1% growth of Airbnb, hotels are impacted by half a percent.[9]

Big brands too are utilising technology to create value-driven experiences to engage customers and reach new audiences. Many have optimised their value chains and created new products or services to take advantage of new systems of exchange. Outdoor brand Patagonia's partnership with eBay, to create an e-commerce peer-to-peer marketplace for pre-owned branded clothing, has tapped into this community. Car manufacturer Ford has responded by launching its own car-sharing service, FORD2GO. Walmart has launched Game Trade, where video game owners can trade their games with each other, and W Hotels are partnering with DesksNear.Me to provide rented business spaces for their guests.

It would seem that everything that's old is new again, and in the case of collaborative consumption this value-driven economic model has had a makeover and it's now

---

8   Serena Saitto, 'Airbnb Said to Be Raising Funding at $20 Billion Valuation', Bloomberg Business, 28 February 2015

9   Jeremiah Owyang, 'Disruption From The Collaborative Economy', 24 September 2014

seriously sexy. From travel to taxis, likeminded individuals are driving empowered consumerism through online marketplaces, and in the process highly capitalised startups are changing traditional market dynamics. Interestingly, the idea of access over ownership isn't an entirely new concept. Public libraries, which have been around for centuries, are a great example of open access – in this case to knowledge – over private ownership. Libraries solve the very modern challenge of sustainability of resources and deliver cost savings in the process. Recently, and to my surprise, libraries have made it into the realm of sexy – using technology to empower their customers by guiding them to access their immense offerings online.

04

Generation Next

As marketers, we've been talking about Millennials (Generation Y) for over a decade now, and the fact is they've grown up and many now have children. Importantly, Millennials have come of age and now represent a very large share of spending power in the economy. It follows that this spending power will only increase as their earnings grow. Born between 1980 and 2000, Millennials have grown up in an era of rapid technological advancement; they are the first digital-native generation. With everything at their fingertips they're global and super-connected, their purchasing behaviour differs from the generations that preceded them. They are early adopters of new products and services and very influential within their peer groups.

Largest share of wallet

According to Nielsen, the Millennial generation makes up 24% of the US population and at 77 million people that's on par with Baby Boomers. Australian researcher and forecaster McCrindle's analysis shows this generation represents 22%[10] – as do Baby Boomers[11] – of Australia's 23 million population.[12] By 2025, this generation will be 31% of the Australian workforce, representing the consumer segment with the largest share of wallet.[13] Many businesses will therefore need to rethink their brand, marketing and business models in order to meet Millennials' needs. Research indicates that the negative stereotyping of Millennials has prevented some brands from forming strong relationships with them, and in many cases shows executives 'who make product and service decisions for their companies have negative or dismissive attitudes towards Millennials'.[14]

While negative perceptions such as 'lazy' and 'self-entitled' may be influencing how executives view this generation, research on Millennials defines them as an optimistic generation that are fast adopters of technology, engaged in consuming and influencing, and believing that business and government can bring about global change. This is the generation that 'engages with brands extensively, personally and emotionally – and in entirely different ways – than have other generations'.[15] Marketing savvy, they expect aligned brand values such as being authentic and

10   Australia's Generational Profile, McCrindle Website, 2014

11   Ibid

12   Ibid

13   Ibid

14   'The Millennial Consumer: Debunking the Myths', Boston Consulting Group, 2012

15   Barton, Koslow, Beuchamp, bcg perspectives, 'How Millennials Are Changing the Face of Marketing Forever', Boston Consulting Group, 15 January 2014

transparent, a two-way reciprocal relationship in which they feel that brands are part of their lives, and – because they're digitally connected – they share absolutely everything, including brand recommendations, opinions and feedback. And while they will happily 'like' and recommend positive experiences to their friends and peers, the reverse is true for negative ones, leading to online criticism in reviews, blogs and social media.

Marketing to Millennials

In marketing, as in pop culture, Millennials are leading indicators of large-scale changes in future consumer behaviour. 'They are influencing and accelerating shifts in consumer attitudes, spending habits, and brand perceptions and preferences even among Gen-Xers and Baby Boomers. As a result, this generational transition is ushering in the end of consumer marketing as we have long known it.'[16] For brands this is a transition from push marketing controlled by the organisation to two-way, collaborative and participative customised experiences. Millennials are (more than any other generation) smartphone and multi-device connected, and they like engaging with brands through social media and their mobile phones. The new age of brand engagement is interactive in a multichannel, multi-device ecosystem; to this generation the brand

---

16   Barton, Koslow, Beuchamp, bcg perspectives, 'How Millennials Are
       Changing the Face of Marketing Forever', Boston Consulting Group,
       15 January 2014

experience is just one seamless channel of which they are a part.

Importantly, to develop deep connections with this generation, brands need to demonstrate their aligned values in order to craft meaningful connections. Millennials see brands as drivers of social change with the power to unite people behind social responsibility. They want brands to be purpose-led and active in supporting social causes that are relevant to their industry. Millennials are willing to support brands with social causes, because it's what they believe in and care about; they're looking to brands to authentically make a difference.

Millennials are becoming the heartbeat of consumer culture; they are informed, connected and sceptical of advertising. The challenge for marketers will be to develop super-creative ways that this generation will want to share brand messaging with their peers; that is, content that's so good it is shared ahead of an inspirational quote or a funny meme.

05

Always On

Digital-first marketplaces have changed the relationship between brands and customers. Fast, personable, solution-providing service is the expectation of today's customer. Consumers expect brands to deliver a customer experience that is timely, accessible and seamless. People are now super-connected and have 365/24/7 access to brands through social media and online channels. What they expect is real-time access, helpful responses to their enquiries and solutions to their problems at a time and in a channel that suits them.

Ten years ago an irate customer would have called a customer service manager, fired off an angry email and discussed their negative brand experience with their family and friends over a coffee. Today, their voice of discontent is much, much louder, with disgruntled customers broadcasting their unfavourable stories of dissatisfaction in their social media networks, communicating with their peers every detail of their experience, culminating in damaging brand discussions and negative customer opinion. Most pressing for brands is managing their brand reputation online, as pre-purchase decision-making often involves online research, in which negative reviews impact significantly on whether the customer purchases or not.

Not happy!

Recently, a friend of mine embarked on a six-day Facebook rant regarding the loss of his family's luggage. His posts reminded me of a British Airways customer service incident gone very wrong on social media. The case of the Chicago-based businessman using a *paid* tweet to deliver a two-day reputational sting to the British Airways brand highlights the new power to the customer world and the lengths that disgruntled customers are willing to go to if they're not being heard.

The promoted 60-character tweet read, 'Don't fly with @British_Airways. They can't keep track of your luggage'. Calling out bad service in social media has become more commonplace, however it's the first time a customer has used Twitter's self-serve promoted tweet platform and paid to promote a tweet to tens of thousands of Twitter users. Using $1,000 of his own cash, this frustrated and now famous British Airways customer promoted his complaint. Within hours the airline responded with a personal apology and the recovery of his luggage. Meanwhile, news outlets had picked up the story and, aided by mainstream media coverage, his tweets went viral, allowing thousands more people to experience his frustration. Data shows that '89 percent of consumers began doing business with a competitor following a poor customer experience and 79 percent of consumers who shared complaints about poor customer experience online had their complaints ignored'.[17]

Online customer opinions, reviews and recommendations have radically shifted the customer's path-to-purchase, with satisfied customers influencing the purchase behaviour of new customers. Nielsen Research shows that online reviews are the second most trusted source of brand information, with 70% of global respondents saying they trusted information from the customer channel.[18]

Customers are leveraging the power of their social networks to broadcast their dissatisfaction, making their customer experience true for not only the brand but for a broader audience too. This has forced brands to adapt very quickly and use technology to activate digital and social customer service channels which enable the customer and the brand to participate in a two-way, real-time, online conversation and to answer questions, respond quickly to enquires and solve problems.

Today's new customer service model for brands is 'always on', where empowered customers use technology to interact with brands anytime and anywhere – and

17 'Getting to the Heart of the Consumer and Brand Relationship', Customer Experience Impact Report, Oracle, 2011

18 Nielsen 'Global Trust in Advertising' Report, 2013

they're using these channels to speak out when brands don't listen. Today, as never before, customer experience is the brand.

06

The Business Case

Businesses today operate in a highly competitive and commoditised marketplace, plagued by political and economic uncertainty. Customer relationships have traditionally been built on the back of transactional marketing practices such as sales discounting, promotions and merchandising. These transactional marketing practices offer little or no competitive difference, deliver low customer advocacy, and are low involvement, one-dimensional experiences, are easily replaced by competing offers where there's little difference in the eyes of the customer between one offering and the next.

As competition increases, transactional marketing practices such as these will become unsustainable, leaving brands to differentiate on customer experience. For this reason, brands are putting customer experience on their agenda with an organisational focus on positive brand experiences that foster satisfaction where the customer is 'likely to purchase 17.5% more from them'[19] than organisations that are customer experience laggards.

The brand amplifier

Advocacy results from positive brand interactions that lead to customer satisfaction – advocacy occurs when the value of the brand experience is discussed and the brand is then recommended. Increasingly, customer advocacy has a pivotal role in influencing purchase behaviour. According to *Forbes*, '80% of all purchases include some form of word-of-mouth recommendation during the purchase cycle.'[20] For brands operating in the experience economy today, advocacy has inherent value, representing market share growth, future revenues and profitability.

The connection between what's experienced and whether the customer advocates is explicitly linked. Research shows that word-of-mouth is influential in driving purchasing decisions and this is influenced directly by customer experience. Simply put, when a customer has a positive brand experience and their functional needs are met, the customer is likely to proactively recommend the brand.

Today, customers are very quick to express their satisfaction or dissatisfaction with their brand/customer interactions, and it is this which is impacting the purchasing

---

19   'The Ultimate Customer Experience', Customer Experience Matters, Temkin, 7 October 2014

20   'Improve Customer Acquisition with an Engagement Strategy', Marketo

behaviour of their peers. When a customer has a negative brand experience the impact of a *single* negative experience has a 'four to five times greater relative impact than a positive one,'[21] giving customers the opportunity to vote with their wallets, taking their business to competitors and in many cases making their negative views public.

Brand influencers

Traditionally, marketers have allocated much of their marketing budget to advertising, which heavily influences audiences at the consideration stage of the purchase journey. Caught up in a never-ending marketing cycle of new customer acquisition, with accelerating costs and high customer churn, research from Bain & Company shows that in many industries, the cost of new customer acquisition is six to seven times higher than the cost of customer retention.[22]

For marketers, the challenge lies in realigning their strategies to the touchpoints of greatest influence in the path-to-purchase. Customers now make their purchasing decisions with on-demand access to an overwhelming quantity of information via a massive number of channels. Access to information is easier and faster than at any other time, and new customers are using these channels to research, review and compare one brand over the next.

---

21   A Pulido, D Stone, J Strevel, 'The Three Cs of Customer Satisfaction: Consistency, Consistency, Consistency,' McKinsey & Company, March 2014

22   'Improve Customer Acquisition with an Engagement Strategy', Marketo

Unlike customers of the past, today's satisfied customer continues to engage with the brand post-purchase through channels such as social media, driving a continuous loop of engagement and advocacy through word-of-mouth recommendations. From real-world conversations in cafes to online posts, reviews and discussion forums, customers are sharing their opinions with other people and providing accessible information for new customers throughout the purchase journey. These are the new sources of product/service information that is considered credible and trustworthy, and are very influential in shoppers' purchasing decisions.

In this era of advertising scepticism, brand advocacy has inherent business value and according to Nielsen, 'people are *four* times more likely to purchase when referred by a family member or friend.'[23] When a customer makes a positive word-of-mouth recommendation to a family member, friend, co-worker or their social network, they are expressing their satisfaction with the brand experience, which is one of the most powerful influences in helping a new customer along the path-to-purchase.

As marketers realise the value of word-of-mouth recommendations, brands will increasingly begin to shift more of their marketing spend from advertising and promotions to the stages in the purchase journey that influence and drive advocacy. Word of Mouth Marketing Association (WOMMA) research points to one offline word-of-mouth

---

23   Nielsen 'Global Trust in Advertising and Brand Messages', 2013

impression driving at least five times more sales than one paid media impression, with offline word-of-mouth amplifying the effect of paid media by 15%.[24]

Top performer

An Australian-owned brand that has put advocacy on the top of their business agenda is telecommunications company Telstra. The brand has a steadfast commitment to customer-first experiences, believing that customer advocacy underpins the growth of the business, making impacting the lifetime value of their customers a key driver of business growth.

As an ongoing measure of brand health and customer relationships, Telstra developed a Net Promoter Score attribution modelling approach to understanding customer behaviour such as engagement which has been applied to all customer analytics. Furthermore, 'Telstra is able to record NPS across 30,000 customers on average',[25] which is attributed to their individual customer records. NPS has enabled the marketing team 'to look at value pools and to be able to create the right types of offerings that [they] can take to market and deliver to people in a way that's relevant to their needs'.[26]

---

24   'Return On Word Of Mouth', WOMMA, 2014

25   Nadia Cameron, 'How Telstra is Applying Data Analytics to Customer Experience', CMO.com, 5 May 2015

26   Nadia Cameron, 'Telstra's Inese Kingsmill Shares how Customer Advocacy is Elevating Marketing's Role', CMO.com, 17 February 2015

Telstra's Head of Corporate Marketing, Inese Kingsmill has been pivotal in the business shift from an engineering company to an organisation that's marketing led. Marketing represents the customer's agenda, and the brand's products and services are now developed to provide a better customer experience. Underpinning Telstra's customer-centric culture and marketing stewardship is the building of sophisticated research, insights and analytics systems and processes. This has enabled the company to understand the drivers of advocacy and identify value pools to improve business growth.

While advocacy levels vary from category to category, Boston Consulting Group's research on word-of-mouth indicates that there isn't a category in which customer advocacy is irrelevant. Their analysis showed 'that the revenue growth of the brands with the highest advocacy levels is far above the industry average. Over time, that difference separates the leaders from the laggards.'[27]

As the marketplace evolves and the expectations of customers continue to increase, brands will need to shift their focus from product to customer-centricity, where customer satisfaction leading to advocacy becomes a whole-of-business approach, encompassing people, processes and systems. This will be the point at which the customer is recognised as the most important asset of the organisation and their advocacy will determine the health of the brand.

---

27   Pedro Esquivias, Steve Knox, Victor Sánchez-Rodríguez and Jody
      Visser, bcg perspectives, 'Fueling Growth Through Word of Mouth',
      Boston Consulting Group, 2 December 2013

Part Two

THE 7 PILLARS OF CUSTOMER EXPERIENCE

07

Where to Begin

Some brand leaders are beginning to realise that customer experiences are the brand, however many haven't realised it – yet. According to Forrester Research, 'Over the next decade, literally every company will compete on the basis of customer experience. In fact, they already do – most just don't realise what that really means, what's at stake, or how to do it well.'[28] The experience economy is upon us; great brand experiences that unlock customer value are the experiences that differentiate one brand from the next and drive competitive advantage.

When the competition are all selling the same message – lowest prices everyday; guaranteed lowest price or your money back, or buy this to win! – the question for marketers is: will their customers continue to see these tactics as a point of differentiation let alone competing brands delivering rewarding experiences? For some brands, shifting their marketing strategy from price/product to customer

---

28   Harley Manning & Kerry Bodine, *Outside In: The Power of Putting Customers at the Centre of Your Business*, Forrester Research, 22 May 2012

experience will be perceived as risky business. Brand leaders at executive level will need to analyse their brand's reputation, market share, customer loyalty, culture and business systems and processes before embarking on the transformation to customer-first, where the needs of their customers are met at every brand/customer interaction.

Start with the customer

Creating a competitive advantage on the back of customer experience may be less daunting than it first appears. The journey begins with the premise that the customer has evolved; now everything is at their fingertips, they're global and super-connected through their social networks, their purchasing behaviours have changed, they're early adopters of technology and switched on 24/7. What comes next is shaping the strategy and future direction of the brand, where marketing has a seat at the table with input on the business agenda from the customer's perspective. These are the conversations and actions that start the transformation from a brand that is product/service centric to a brand that is customer first and marketing led.

What will inform the next stage is access to customer data. Some organisations will have already built cross-organisation capabilities around research, insights and analytics. For many, this data will be siloed across their business, and for others, their business will still operate from base-level customer information. The importance of customer data is high; at an entry level, brands need to understand their customers' needs by measuring customer satisfaction and customer recommendations, listening to customers' brand conversations online and mapping the path-to-purchase to understand their pain points and the gaps in the brand offering.

For marketers embarking on transformation I believe there are 7 *Pillars of Customer Experience* that form the foundation to building deeper relationship connections across all areas of the brand to create higher emotional engagement that fosters customer satisfaction and advocacy.

The 7 Pillars of Customer Experience

1   **Brand Purpose** is the 'why' behind the brand, why it exists and what it stands for; its reason for being and its belief. Purpose provides meaning and focus within an organisation, it defines the brand's role in culture, and how people will connect with it, and importantly purpose provides an authentic narrative. Ultimately, purpose is the deepest expression of a brand, providing understanding of how the brand impacts the wider community. Importantly, it unites the customer and the organisation's culture in pursuit of its intention.

2   **Organisational Alignment** is the best way to ensure that all divisions within the business are aligned in delivering great customer experiences. Alignment brings together marketing, customer service, sales,

IT, HR and operations within a customer-first culture, ensuring there are no gaps between what is promised by the brand and what is delivered to the customer. Many organisations will find cultural alignment around the delivery of customer experiences challenging. Organisational leaders will need to foster a customer-first mindset, coupled with the collaboration of internal stakeholders, to bring together operational data, CRM databases and customer feedback, and ensure there is a closed-loop sharing of intelligence.

3   **Customer Journey** mapping is a powerful tool to understand the customer purchase journey. Mapping the brand touchpoints from the customer's perspective helps marketers understand how customers are interacting with the brand. A journey map represents the brand/customer interactions in each channel as the customer experiences it, including their online search, website research, in-store visits, online purchasing behaviour, social media discussions and customer service interactions. The process helps understand customers' needs and expectations at each brand intersection. Using topline data, customer feedback, one-on-one interviews, focus groups and ethnography the process clarifies customer needs, behaviour, perspectives, and moments-of-truth. The process serves as a framework

for designing and optimising the brand's touchpoints to minimise gaps and customer pain points.

4   **Keeping the Promise** is what is expected in every interaction with the brand. A brand promise signifies the value that is created by the brand when the customer engages with the product or service. The more clearly the promise is articulated across the customer touchpoints and folded into the experience the more likely the brand is to be perceived as authentic, true to its values and fulfilling its customer needs. Organisations need to align the whole of the organisation, its culture, systems and processes, to effectively deliver the brand promise in every channel to foster customer satisfaction and advocacy.

5   **Technology** is providing people with access to information anytime and anywhere they choose. Innovation is set to intensify, as smart, connected products emerge, triggering more innovation, higher productivity, sustained economic growth and a new era of competition. Brands now have the capability to collect personal data such as location, language, times of interaction and purchase preferences to create rich customer profiles that predict their real-time needs to deliver personalised and seamless experiences. Technology and social platforms are driving new economic models around empowered consumerism called 'collaborative consumption', where goods and

services are accessed rather than privately owned. Waiting in the wings are the early adopters of the latest technologies, such as robotics and 3D printing, where people in the not-too-distant future will design and customise products to suit their own personal preferences. The marketing reality is that people are continuously connected, using their smart devices to access and connect on their terms, and this is changing how people are experiencing brands.

6   **Co-creation** is the practice of engaging and involving customers and brand fans in seeking knowledge, strategic insights, problem-solving solutions, innovation and design. This is where customers are actively involved in product or service innovation and joint creation of value to deliver improvement in existing offerings or create new ideas from which both the organisation and the customer derives value. Co-creation draws together groups of diverse individuals with the potential to solve business challenges of all kinds and effectively encourages active participation to create richer experiences.

7   **Experience Management** and measurement necessitates deep understanding of the relationship between customer behaviour and the experience. Experience management aims to provide a single view of the customer experience across interactions, channels, products and services, and time. Leading indicators from different data sources measure the

performance and business value generated from systematic improvements in customer experience and how this directly impacts customer satisfaction and advocacy.

08

Pillar One: Brand Purpose

Marketers who have the ambition to create meaningful brand/customer connections need look no further than the master of 'why a brand exists', Simon Sinek. Described as a leading visionary thinker, Sinek has written and spoken extensively about 'why we do what we do'. His 'why' concept is the central tenet for defining brand purpose. 'How Leaders Inspire Great Action'[29] explains the reason that just a handful of brands are able to inspire where others are failing. These organisations know why they exist, their purpose has been weaved into the central fabric of their culture, and they think, act and communicate not from what they do, but why they do it.

The power of why is the purpose, cause or belief that inspires an organisation to do what it does. Sinek uses the example of the technology brand Apple, an organisation with the same access to the same resources, talent, agencies and media as their competitors and yet, year after

---

29   Simon Sinek, 'How Leaders Inspire Great Action', TED, 2009

year, Apple's innovation in technology drives extraordinary financial success. Loyalty to the Apple brand isn't because the business makes great technologies, it's because people believe in what the brand does; it is why Apple fans are happy to queue for hours – or even overnight – for the latest iPhone.

Today, people are increasingly smarter and better informed in their purchasing decisions; it would seem that yesterday's mindless consumption is a thing of the past. In its place, a post-recession customer who's evolved and now has an increasing interest in brands that are delivering value and providing a positive and fundamental impact in and on their lives. These are brands that know their purpose and have an authentic narrative that people believe in. A brand that comes to mind is TOMS Shoes – a business that creates both social and commercial value and that's built on the buy-one–give-one model.

Purpose before profit

The founder of TOMS, Blake Mycoskie, was inspired to start the company after a visit to Argentina where he met children so poor they couldn't afford to buy shoes. His pledge was TOMS would donate one pair of shoes (in developing countries) for every pair sold. Since founding the business in 1996, 'TOMS has donated more than two million pairs of shoes, with approximately one million of those pairs donated in the past two years alone'.

Analysis of the buy-one–give-one model by Stanford Social Innovation Review concludes 'that the buy-one give-one model is not only a viable way to create both commercial and social value but also a model of social entrepreneurship that is likely to increase in prevalence and power. Trends in consumer behaviour, particularly in the Millennial generation, which puts a high value on social issues, along with the model's simple yet effective marketing message, provide a way for companies to leverage their core competencies for a social cause'.[30]

Much more than a marketing lever, 'purpose' is at the core of long-term brand strategy, representing a shift in thinking and a transformation in how a business operates and creates sustainable business growth. When we understand the customer truth we can unlock the brand's purpose; that is, we know what the brand stands for in people's lives. Purpose defines the brand behaviour both internally and through every customer interaction, including its people and culture, product and services, customer service and communications. Purpose provides meaning and focus within an organisation, it defines the brand's role in culture, its reason for being and how people will connect with it. Importantly, purpose provides an authentic narrative.

Higher brand purpose or social purpose is built on an organisation's moral conviction and obligation to do the right thing for business, society and the planet. Jim

---

30   Christopher Marquis & Andrew Park, *Stanford Social Innovation Review*, 'Inside the Buy-One Give-One Model', 2014

Stengel, author of *Grow: How Ideals Power Growth and Profit at the World's Greatest Companies*, is a leader of the movement for creating ideal-driven brands. His point of view is that businesses with higher ideals build deep, authentic relationships that shape brand behaviour, rituals, systems, processes and culture, influencing the communications inside the organisation and impacting the experiences that people have.

In collaboration with research company Millward Brown Optimor, Stengel identified that the key driver of extraordinary financial success was that each organisation had a clearly defined higher ideal purpose as a central tenet of their business strategy. Their research demonstrated how these brands outperformed their competition in brand value and financial growth, with many of the brands maintaining their price premium.[31] Brands include: Google, which exists to immediately satisfy every curiosity; IBM, which exists to help build a smarter planet; Red Bull, which is energising the world; and Coke, which exists to inspire moments of happiness.

Higher purpose brands act with resolve in improving the lives of people; a force for social good that's bigger than profit. These are the brands that craft meaningful connections with powerful ideals; the ideal 'is the brand's reason for being, it explains why the brand exists and the impact it seeks to leave on the world'.[32] In his work with P+G brand

31   'How Brands Drive Value Growth', Millward Brown

32   Jim Stengel, *Grow: How Ideals Power Growth and Profit at the World's Greatest Companies*, 2014

Pampers Nappies, Stengel transitioned the company positioning from 'dry nappies, happy child' to 'caring for happy, healthy development of babies around the world'. This higher purpose galvanised the company, extending the brand from communicating product attributes to partnering with UNICEF to provide newborn vaccines for tetanus and building a global community of likeminded carers to learn about the health and development of babies.

When a brand has a clear higher or social purpose it can ask, *how does it help people live better lives?* In the Pampers case, the brand's impact was not just with their customer or in their customer's world, but the world at large. A recent WARC article, *In Pursuit of Brand Purpose* by Liz Tinlin, describes audience layers as 'Me', 'My World' and 'The World'. A brand that has higher purpose at the brand's heart with the intention of providing greater good operates in the audience space of 'The World'. Tinlin says, '…as soon as you go beyond "Me" and into "My World" or "The World", you are starting to make your brand more sustainable, which – as we all know – is rising to the top of the business agenda.'

Real connection

The personal care category is highly competitive and commoditised; a category dominated by innovation and hybrid products. Personal care brand Dove is the 'poster child' of weaving the brand's social purpose 'to celebrate every woman's unique beauty' into the fabric of the brand.

The purpose provides the brand with an authentic and inspiring connection across the three audience layers ('Me' and into 'My World' or 'The World'). Dove's campaign for Real Beauty was created to stimulate thinking and provoke discussion on how women see themselves; through their eyes and the eyes of others. Its goal was to help women 'develop a positive relationship with beauty, helping to raise their self-esteem and thereby enabling them to realise their full potential.'[33]

In 2004, Dove commissioned a worldwide study, and the subsequent report, 'The Real Truth About Beauty', revealed that the definition of beauty in our culture had 'become limiting and unattainable' and that 'only 2% of women around the world would describe themselves as beautiful'.[34] Ten years on and the brand continues to share its point of view on its role in society, by authentically engaging with women through the latest campaign, Real Beauty Sketches. Dove clearly articulates its purpose to change the wider definition of beauty and improve the self-esteem of women. At the AANA 2014 Conference in Australia, Marc Mathieu, Senior VP of Marketing at Unilever, said, 'Unless we understand human insight, we won't unlock purpose.' The insight on the Dove Real Beauty Sketches: 9 out of 10 women don't think they're beautiful.[35]

Real Beauty Sketches is a three-minute short film giving insight into how women feel about their looks. Each

33   Unilever, Dove, Company Website

34   Dove, Social Mission, Company Website

35   Marc Mathieu, Unileaver, AANA Conference 2014

of the women describes in detail their facial features for an FBI forensic artist; the artist sketches them from behind a curtain. Strangers who have met with these women the previous day are then asked to describe them and the women's portraits are drawn for a second time. The women are invited back into the studio, where the two portraits are compared. In the first sitting, each of the women are critical of aspects of their facial features, whereas the second portrait, drawn from the strangers' viewpoint, shows the women are more beautiful than they believe. The film elicited strong emotional responses from the women involved and viewers alike.

The month after the Dove *Real Beauty Sketches* release, the short film had gained 114 million global views across 110 counties; it was the third most shared video of all time. The brand's corporate website reports that the widespread media coverage across the world has led to celebrities joining the discussion, 121 print features, 484 news and lifestyle segments, and thousands of online articles, blogs, comments, likes and shares. To date, Google reports the campaign has generated 4.6 billion PR blogger media impressions. Mathieu believes that, 'Today we need fundamental human truth as the heart of our brands, and we need to give a point of view. It's that point of view that encourages engagement and if we do a good job, people will embrace it and share it.'[36]

---

36   Marc Mathieu, Unileaver, AANA Conference 2014

Dove has pursued a strategy that both creates business value and delivers on measurable social purpose. The brand transformation from a commoditised range of everyday beauty products on the supermarket shelves to a brand whose story taps into cultural truth and empowers women to embrace their own beauty continues to deliver high-performance business results, with an estimated brand value this year of $4.8 billion, making it one of the most valuable brands in the world.[37]

Global studies are showing that there is a demonstrable relationship between social purpose and sustained business performance, and that brands can in fact have a societal benefit *and* maximise profit and return shareholder value.[38] This alignment is being driven by people making decisions in response to a brand's social purpose. There is a shift in behavioural changes towards brands that are doing good in that, when quality and price are equal, people are making purchasing decisions on a third purchase trigger: purpose. It would seem that purpose is delivering brands a distinct competitive advantage; an advantage that is authentic and meaningful. Evidence over five years shows that, 'Not only are consumers making purchase decisions with Purpose top of mind, they are also buying and advocating for purposeful brands'.[39]

---

37   BrandZ Top 100 Most Valuable Global Brands, Millward Brown, 2014

38   goodpurpose® study, Edelman, 2012

39   Ibid

United by brand purpose

Most importantly, purpose enables business leaders to effect organisational change and improve business performance. This is the type of transformation that requires change from the top, translating the values across the whole of the business. As the organisation reorientates to be purpose-led the culture of the organisation goes through realignment too.

To begin the journey of creating a brand purpose, internal stakeholders will need to understand what purpose is and how it will unite the organisation's culture with its customers. Developing a brand purpose should not be done in isolation, and for this reason, my agency involves key internal stakeholders in contributing to the process of brand understanding right from the start. Employee involvement early in the process adds value through engagement, education and empowerment, providing a sense of ownership that is then championed across the organisation organically. From the process should come a shared belief that shapes every action of the brand.

For marketers inspired to build a strong and enduring purpose-led brand, purpose is not about business objectives, positioning or target audience segmentation. These are performance outcomes and marketing definitions of marketing, and these are not necessarily what your audience or society at large cares about. They care about meaning and brands that have an authentic narrative that sets them apart; they care about transparency and a commitment to making their world and the wider world a better place. This, in turn, is what is providing purpose-led brands with a competitive advantage in a time of brand parity and commoditisation.

09

Pillar Two:
Organisational Alignment

One of the greatest challenges organisations face in customer experience management is overcoming functional silos across marketing, customer service, sales, IT, HR and operations, and the processes and policies across the organisation as a whole. The hardest thing for competitors to copy is the customer experiences an organisation creates. To deliver the value that comes from positive experiences, organisations need to rally their people behind the customer and aggregate this as a single focus behind delivering consistent, total customer experience.

Greatest gains

Some of the greatest customer experience gains can come from within the organisation by having an outside-in, customer-first approach, where the customers' needs are consciously at the centre of every brand/customer interaction. In this scenario the company exists to serve its customers, delivering and keeping the promises made. Numerous studies show that dissatisfied and unengaged employees beget dissatisfied customers, and when a new customer has a negative brand experience, the impact of a *single* negative experience has a '…four to five times greater relative impact than a positive one…'.[40]

Increasingly, organisations are looking to CMOs to step into the role of custodian of the customer relationship, dismantling internal silos to own the conversion pathway across marketing, sales and service to create consistent customer experiences that today's customer expects.

For brand leaders, organisation alignment around a customer-centric culture is a painstaking and lengthy process that requires constant reiteration and high-level commitment across the entire company. Don't get me wrong; it's not the role of the CMO to define the process management, but rather, their responsibility to ensure that each division delivers customer value – legacy system enhancements, cross-function sharing of data, the formation of new teams and new roles, training and education, internal performance metrics and the process of customer service design, to name a few.

Importantly, perceptions of the marketing department will need to shift too, from buzzwords around branding, advertising, promotions and a perceived lack of accountability to custodians of the total customer experience,

40   A Pulido, D Stone, J Strevel, 'The Three Cs of Customer Satisfaction: Consistency, Consistency, Consistency,' McKinsey & Company, 1 March 2014

visibility at the frontline and driving and shaping a growth agenda. An evolution in marketing skills is needed too, from traditional marketing such as brand awareness, managing media and demand generation to providing customer experiences that create value, marketing people and processes will shift to measuring customer satisfaction, customer listening, expanding data management capabilities, managing business process change and strengthening digital skillsets. Importantly, marketing will need the right people, those with broad marketing knowledge combined with a specialisation in data analytics, social, search optimisation, content marketing and behavioural science (the study of decision-making, judgement and human behaviour).

Change makers

As organisations realise the power of creating great customer experiences, silos will be dismantled and CMOs will increasingly own the total customer experience from brand awareness to customer service. For CMOs the evolution of their marketing remit is already underway, with innovation in web to CRM programs, real-time customer feedback, social listening platforms, marketing automation that delivers seamless personalised communications, and tools that deliver rich data on customer/brand interactions.

Organisational leaders will need to foster a customer experience mindset and nurture long-term cultural change. For change to take place, senior leaders will need to collaborate with internal stakeholders and bring together operational data, CRM databases and customer feedback to ensure there is a closed-loop sharing of intelligence company-wide. To effect change, customer experience needs to be on the agenda of the senior leadership team: building the case for customer experience, providing understanding of the benefits and outcomes, ensuring funding, managing technology, developing a voice of the customer program, and measuring and managing the cross-functional systems and processes.

A demonstration of organisational commitment of this magnitude delivers a strong signal to internal stakeholders that the company is fully committed to its customer experience goals. Positioning the transformation as a cross-function rather than a siloed effort enables open communications and transparency between business functions and teamwork, delivering consistency at each touchpoint in the customer journey.

High performance

Customer-centred organisations such as Commonwealth Bank of Australia are outperforming the marketplace with their outside-in approach to customer experience by putting the customer at the core of their business. While this sounds simple enough and many brands are claiming their customer-centricity, the Commonwealth Bank's customer experience strategy is driving high-performance results in this area. The strategy was built on the company's vision of: 'people, technology, strength and productivity.'[41] With customer-centric innovation a priority, the brand formed their Innovation Academy to find new ways to engage customers and drive exceptional experience.

Their goal was big. Ralph Norris – the CEO at the time – said, 'Customer service is our top priority. We plan to invest in the capabilities of our people through reinvigorating our service and sales program and by giving staff greater autonomy to provide customers with solutions directly at the first point of contact.'[42] This company-wide shift to being singular in their focus on customer-first was made possible by a program of cultural, technological and process transformation, aligning all aspects of the bank until the performance outcomes were achieved.

In 2013 the brand launched an extensive campaign to all brand stakeholders. The 'Can' campaign increased awareness of the initiative, helping to shift customer attitudes and delivering the highest number of satisfied customers in Australia. The bank's transformation was a change program 10 years in the making, in uncertain times and in a highly competitive environment. The bank's four-step approach to developing a customer-centric mindset reinvented how the organisation engaged its customers.

In order to create customer experiences that satisfy customers' needs and to deliver the brand promise consistently at each touchpoint, organisations will need to

---

41 CBA's 4 step Plan, 'Developing A customer Centric Mindset', *Inside HR*, 2 September 2013

42 Ibid

connect strategy and operations and align people, systems and data behind their customer experience vision. Internal stakeholders need to collaborate, share and coordinate across the organisation, creating a closed loop to better understand customer needs and how to best serve these customers.

10

Pillar Three:
Customer Journey

Most marketers are experiencing a rapid shift in customer purchasing behaviour brought about by our digital-first world: the speed of innovation, disruptive digital technologies, and the changing face of the customer – who is now digitally savvy and super-connected with evolving buying behaviours. Today, the customer purchase journey is complex and bridges both the physical and the digital, with almost limitless channels for online search, research and purchasing. By 2016 it is expected that online 'will influence more than half of *all* retail transactions, representing a potential sales opportunity of almost $2 trillion.'[43]

Organisations collectively are spending billions of dollars on experiences that are designed to attract and retain customers. Retailers are building new stores and sophisticated e-commerce websites and digital applications, social

---

43   E Bramble, D Edelman, K Ungerman, 'Digitising The Customer Journey', McKinsey & Company, June 2014

platforms are being utilised by brands for anywhere, any-time customer service, marketing automation programs are now personalising electronic communications and market-ers are experimenting with new channels for paid, earned and owned marketing. The number of brand touchpoints has been super-sized over the past 10 years, and in this hyper-competitive landscape each touchpoint needs to meet the customer's needs and add up to a differentiated total experience.

The new lens

Marketing strategies that were relevant a decade ago are mostly obsolete. In the past, when purchase journeys were linear and media channels were few, much of the market-ing budget was allocated to brand-building awareness which heavily influenced audiences at consideration and then point-of-purchase. Many organisations still continue to view customer purchase behaviour through this lens of the traditional purchase funnel, not accounting for how the path-to-purchase is being influenced by the vast num-ber of touchpoints, information anytime and anywhere, and rapidly evolving technology.

Coupled with these new-world marketing challenges are diminishing levels of satisfaction from organisations at the response rates of marketing efforts: 'sixty-five (65%) or more of marketing leaders are dissatisfied with results.'[44]

---

44   Tony Zambito, 'The CMP Modern Marketing Guide to Buyer Personas and Buyer Insights Research (Part 3)', Customer Think, 2014

This has led marketers to realign their strategies and budgets to where customers are now spending their time in the purchase journey. Marketers are fast becoming responsible for the entire customer journey, from the first search to the 'moment-of-truth' when the customer purchases a product or service. Brands are shifting their focus from singular touchpoints and are instead investing in understanding the total experience across multiple touchpoints and in multiple channels over time and from the customer perspective. Additionally, 'maximizing satisfaction with customer journeys has the potential not only to increase customer satisfaction by 20 percent but also to lift revenue by up to 15 percent while lowering the cost of serving customers by as much as 20 percent.'[45]

Mapping the journey

Customer journey mapping is the process of describing the customer journey through each of the customer/brand interactions. The journey is mapped from the customer's perspective and emphasises the influential touchpoints between the customer and the brand. Mapping is a strategic tool that captures key insights into complex customer behaviour and delivers greater clarity around the customer's needs at each intersection; the gaps, pain points, moments-of-truth and where the opportunities lie for touchpoint optimisation and improvement. Mapping

---

45   A Pulido, D Stone, J Strevel, 'The Three Cs of Customer Satisfaction: Consistency, Consistency, Consistency,' McKinsey & Company, 1 March 2014

the entire customer journey for each behavioural customer segment is creating a detailed roadmap for increasing customer satisfaction, managing churn and aligning internal processes.

The process of mapping the customer's path-to-purchase builds customer intelligence and consensus cross-functionally within an organisation, delivering deeper understanding from a human-centred perspective and shifting thinking from singular touchpoints to total experience. Due to changes in purchasing behaviours the need for organisations to deeply understand their customers' evolving purchasing behaviours is growing, and this is presenting new challenges that require new approaches.

To deliver this, marketers need access to customer data from across their organisation that is most often held in the vertical functions of the business. This is critical customer information that is siloed across many business functions – including marketing, sales, customer service and IT – denying internal stakeholders a holistic view of each stage of the journey and a clear picture of the total customer experience.

The process of mapping the customer journey requires collaboration across the organisation for deeper collective understanding of the customer's purchase journey. At my agency, our approach is to involve internal stakeholders from across the business. Involving cross-functional teams in the mapping process creates direct customer empathy and builds consensus among those who can effect the greatest change. Additionally, deeper customer needs insights enable organisations to make better investments into the optimisation of existing touchpoints or the design of new interactions.

Customer journey mapping pieces together the big picture of how and why customers are interacting with the different channels and touchpoints in their path-to-purchase, and will differ depending on whether the brand falls into a high-involvement decision-making process such as buying a motor vehicle or spontaneous decision-making such as purchasing bread or milk. Buying daily, low-evolvement products such as milk and bread the purchase journey is virtually non-existent and is based on habit-driven behaviour, in comparison to buying a motor vehicle where the purchaser would usually spend a long period in market and interact with many touchpoints in the path-to-purchase.

The process

The process of mapping is varied and dependent on the organisation's market share, brand promise, products/ services and usage, audience, communication strategy and customer on-boarding. It is also advantageous to include the company's internal stakeholders in the mapping process. The process uses existing operational customer data, employee insights, customer satisfaction surveys, social media listening, website analytics and – budget permitting – ethnography (observation of how the customer navigates the purchase journey: what they do, see and say) to understand the customer experience. 'Best-in-class companies are using regression models to understand which journeys have the greatest impact on overall customer satisfaction and business outcomes, and then running simulations to get a picture of the potential impact of various initiatives.'[46]

This research and discovery process is essential in capturing the customer story for each customer type. Traditionally, marketers have utilised audience segmentations – based upon demographics, psychographics and purchasing behaviours – to develop their communications strategies to reach target customers with a brand message. However, as customers' buying behaviours have evolved their needs are more precisely defined through the development of personas rather than through demographic data. Personas are built from small-scale qualitative research based on the brand's target audience, and provide insights into attitude and behavioural patterns in purchasing, technology, brand usage and lifestyle, regardless of demographic data.

Journey mapping is a complex process and a framework is critical to analysing the customer data. As specialists in the field, Adaptive Path's methodology uses the building blocks of 'Doing, Thinking and Feeling' coupled with the contextual experiences of 'Place, Time, Device and Relationships'. The framework provides a process to guide the research and analysis of critical information for each of the customer types.

46   A Rawson, E Duncan, C Jones, 'The Truth About Customer Experience', *Harvard Business Review*, September 2013

Once the purchase journey mapping has identified the influential touchpoints, gaps, customer pain points and moments-of-truth, companies are often surprised at customers' brief interactions with the brand and their brand's lack of direct influence on critical purchasing decisions. Many times the touchpoints that are presumed influential by the business are really not. The process will turn up both quick-fix wins and problems that are endemic. There's often many more buyer interactions than were first realised, and the customer journey is far more complex than first assumed, with many of the customer interactions involving multiple cross-operational procedures where things can go wrong. There are also times the purchase journey at a local level will differ in international markets.

The travel map

In line with changing purchasing behaviours of travellers, 30-year-old Australian-based travel brand Flight Centre has undertaken organisational-wide transformation from travel agent to travel retailer. According to CMO.com the travel brand has a greater focus on customer experience with a service-centric process that influences the travel path-to-purchase. The brand has invested in customer journey mapping to better understand their customers across the entire purchasing journey. Insights from the mapping are strengthening marketing's capabilities, along with creating clear product propositions, building an expert customer service workforce and developing an always-on experience for today's traveller.

The brand's GM of Product, Advertising and Experience, Darren Wright, commented: 'The first step was gaining a better picture of what our customers looked like with the intention to understand the customers' behaviour, their profiles, purchasing patterns and general interactions across the Flight Centre portfolio of brands.' Wright said: 'We needed to understand and get a clear position of who our customers were, what formats they like to be spoken to through and how they like to transact with us.'[47] As part of the brand's revitalised customer focus, six new senior executive marketing roles have been created to include customer experiences, loyalty and product.

Realignment

To be effective, journey maps need to reflect the culture and language of the brand. Journey maps should be easy to understand and shared across the business to begin to close the gaps, lift performance and optimise existing or design new touchpoints. It's also a temptation for leaders within the business to prescribe solutions in a top-down approach to remedying the problems identified, when the process requires bottom-up engagement and collaboration to realign cross-functional issues. To that end, many companies that have been studied 'set up a central change

---

47   Nadia Cameron, 'How Flight Centre is Mapping out a New Kind of Customer Journey', CMO.com, 15 January 2015

leadership team with an executive-level head to steer the design and implementation and to ensure that the organisation can break away from functional biases that have historically blocked change.'[48] Additionally, delivering total customer experience at scale requires more than optimising and designing touchpoints, and will take an organisation-wide commitment to customer-centricity, new processes and systems, and metrics to measure performance.

The digital-first marketplace is driving rapid change across the business landscape. Brands that are embracing total customer experience, taking action to understand the customer purchase journey, and making improvements to better meet customer needs are brands that realise their competitive advantage lies in creating relevant, simple, feel-good moments at every brand/customer interaction, because what the customer experiences is remembered and promoted. Marketers are the new custodians of total customer experience, and what's required is a leadership position to ensure that every moment delivers the brand promise across every touchpoint in the customer journey.

---

48   A Rawson, E Duncan, C Jones, 'The Truth About Customer Experience', *Harvard Business Review*, September 2013

11

Pillar Four:
Keeping the Promise

There are no truer words spoken than those by Coca-Cola's President Muhtar Kent, who says, 'If a good brand is a promise, then a great brand is a promise kept.'

A great brand promise connects a brand's purpose, value and positioning to articulate what the customer can expect to receive in their interactions with the brand. Sometimes articulated in a brand's strapline, a promise signifies the value that's created by a brand when the customer engages with the product or service. While brand purpose inspires an organisation to do what it does, the promise delivers the value in the experience; that is, what the brand is committed to delivering. The more clearly the promise is articulated across the customer touchpoints and folded into the customer experience, the more likely the brand is to be perceived as authentic to its values, and with stronger emotional connection comes differentiation.

The delivery gap

While brands aspire to have a loyal tribe of customers that are aligned by higher brand ideals, most often the opposite is true. It would seem that today's marketer is well versed in creating brand promises, but not as good at keeping them. Highly skilled and fully resourced, many marketers can have at their fingertips the tools, processes and talent to help shape brand understanding, define their brand's positioning, interpret complex data, create insight-led brand engagement programs and innovate in the digital space. But marketers need to pay close attention to disparities in what promises the brand makes and what customers experience. A study by management consulting company Bain calls this disparity the 'delivery gap'. In a study of over 350 companies, Bain found that 80% believe their firm offers a superior proposition. However, only 8% of customers held that same view.[49]

Today's marketers' greatest opportunity is to drive organisational value and ensure that the brand keeps its promises. Most organisations are not built to deliver great experiences, with their siloed cultures and legacy systems and processes. What's needed now is an outside-in customer-centred approach, closed-loop intelligence where customer data feeds back into customer improvement actions, organisational agility to navigate and manage the

---

49   Michael Krigsman, 'Bridging The Gap Between Brand Promise and Customer Experience', ZDNet, 1 June 2014

gap between delivery and customers' feedback, and cross-functional systems and processes.

The relationship between marketing and the customer is increasingly complex. Technology-driven shifts in customer behaviour, a question of brand motivation and the role that brands play in people's lives translates into marketers not always being in sync with what customers want or expect. Millward Brown research shows what's important in people's lives is much as expected: safety, children's education, income and work/life balance. However, when it came to brands, respondents didn't rate them top of mind in terms of importance. When asked about their brand choices the important factors were 'what they deemed the brand to stand for, the product experience and what they know of the company behind the brand.'[50]

Food with integrity

The US fast food brand Chipotle Mexican Grill has turned the category upside down with its purpose before profit business model. In doing so, the brand has tapped into what's important in brand choices: purpose, experience and trust. The Chipotle brand story has noble beginnings, with a vision to change the way people think about eating fast food. As the business began to expand, founder Steve Ells's interest turned to how food in the US was produced and processed – partnering with producers to deliver

---

50   'Helping Marketers Get It Right With Consumers', Project Reconnect, World Federation of Advertisers (WFA) and Firefly Milliard Brown

responsible, respectful and sustainable ways to prepare, serve and consume food.

Chipotle's brand promise of 'Food With Integrity' is a philosophy that not only runs throughout the entire organisation but is delivered across every brand and customer interaction. The company delivers their promise through their commitment to searching for better quality and sustainable sources for ingredients and better cooking methods for their foods. Ells says, 'This commitment allows us to keep serving better tasting food all the time.' However, over time, people have started to become more interested in where their food was coming from and how it was produced.

Back to the start

Chipotle first created industry controversy and generated a lot of media attention with its branded content videos: 'Back to the Start' – raising awareness of food practices in an entertaining way; 'Scarecrow' – the company's stand against genetically modified foods; and 'Farmed and Dangerous' – a comedy series that highlights food industry issues. Chris Arnold, Chipotle's Communications Director, says, '…we are trying to solve a problem that many people don't know exists. Although people in the Sustainable Brands community have an above average knowledge of these issues, mainstream consumers often don't understand the differences in how food is raised. This makes our communications challenges two-fold: telling people what Chipotle is doing and why it matters and also building awareness/educating people about the issues, why they matter and demonstrating what Chipotle is doing to make improvements.'[51]

Physical experiences

For these reasons, Arnold admits that marketing sustainable practices through traditional channels such as advertising is difficult. As discussed later in Pillar Six: Co-creation, a strategy that's increasingly being used by brands to foster meaningful connection and deeper engagement is the creation of communities. Creating a community brings customers together through sharing a common experience and develops a deep sense of togetherness, galvanising the brand's promise and its value. Chipotle's signature event 'Cultivate' is an outdoor family festival that celebrates good food and music and draws up to 40,000 people. The festival provides an entertaining and fun experience to highlight and educate people on the work of the Cultivate Foundation, with people coming away from the festival with a clearer understanding of sustainability issues.

At every brand/customer intersection Chipotle creates a brand experience, whether it's in the digital space with their short films, creating communities of likeminded people, partnering with industry bodies such as Farm Aid

51   Mike Hower, 'Run Up to SB'12: An Interview with Chris Arnold of Chipotle', Sustainable Brands, 28 May 2012

and the Land Institute, or using branded physical spaces in their restaurants.

Traditionally, packaging in fast food restaurants is utilised to promote their menus, however Chipotle has always used its cups and bags differently to its competitors, as a means of changing the way people think about food in an entertaining way. Evolving this tradition, Chipotle created the 'Cultivating Thought Author Series'.

It began when bestselling author Jonathan Safran Foer was sitting in a Chipotle restaurant, realising he'd forgotten to bring his book. The thought struck him that it would be great if Chipotle's cups and bags carried thought-provoking cultural ideas from influential people, enabling customers to connect with the musings of writers, comedians and thought-leaders. Foer said, 'We live in a world in which there is shrinking space for literature and writing, and less time than ever for quiet reflection…The idea of expanding the space and time, of creating a small pocket of thoughtfulness right in the middle of the busy day, was inspiring to me – particularly given the size and diversity of the audience, which is America itself.'[52]

The hard reality

The reality is that brands not only need to continually reiterate their brand promise at every customer touchpoint but deliver on their brand promises too. For Chipotle,

---

52   Chipotle Website

their brand promise is not just a platform to leverage marketing tactics. Their purpose runs throughout the whole organisation and its culture, and is driven top down from a higher ideal – it has built a strong reputation for trying to make the world a better place. Their customers eat at the fast food chain because they love the food and share the values of the brand, and they're willing to pay a little more for the experience. And if this isn't evidence enough of, 'If a good brand is a promise, then a great brand is a promise kept,' Chipotle reported a year-to-date, third-quarter 2014 revenue increase of 31.1%, an operating margin of 28.8%, and more than a 50% increase in earnings per share.[53]

Punching above her weight

Back in Australia, entrepreneur Michelle Bridges – best known for her appearances on the TV show *The Biggest Loser* – now presides over a $60 million body transformation and nutrition business empire. According to BRW, her online weight-loss program – the Michelle Bridges 12 Week Body Transformation (12WBT) – has catapulted her into the BRW Rich Women's List with a net worth of $53 million.[54]

Back in 2010, despite her *Biggest Loser* profile, her 12 Week Program had just 1000 signups. Fast-forward to today and it's widely speculated that the last marketing campaign had over 30,000 program sign-ups, with an

---

53   Investor Relations, Chipotle Website
54   Rich Women, *BRW*, 2015

estimated 200,000 members at $200 for each membership since inception.[55]

The brand's phenomenal success can be attributed to: a scalable online business model enabling everyday people access to the 12WBT – anywhere, at anytime and on any device; a brand with purpose, meaning and a commitment to delivering the brand promise; and leveraging the power of word-of-mouth recommendation though social media.

Bridges' brand promise is simple – 'she will support you and be your mate through the process'[56] – and from reading hundreds of online reviews about the program the brand promise is delivered: '…the support team are always there to answer your questions within 24 hours', '…the program offered flexible daily dietary and exercise plans', 'I can access everything on my mobile', '…she keeps me motivated', '…I've fallen in love with this fitness plan', to mention just a few.

What sets Bridges apart from her competitors is the brand delivers its promised value at each brand/customer interaction; that is, her brand delivers to expectation every time, and this in turn creates brand trust. Her customers are highly engaged and satisfied, which drives a continuous loop of engagement and advocacy through word-of-mouth recommendations, and in doing so influences the purchase behaviour of new customers.

55   Jordon Baker, 'Michelle Bridges Found Success with 12 Week Body Transformation', *The Daily Telegraph*, 9 June 2013

56   Ibid

12

Pillar Five: Technology

The influence of technology is changing the way customers are interacting with brands and reshaping the way business is done. Increasingly, organisations are finding their customers now control the brand relationship. As people's digital behaviour evolves, technology is set to play an even greater role in how customers experience brands; the challenge for businesses is to adapt and stay at the forefront of the fast-moving innovations in technology, thereby creating value for their customers through better digital experiences.

Many brands are facing increased competitive pressure from commoditisation and little if any distinct brand differentiation. What is clear is the need for brands to evolve from making and providing more of the same to delivering competitive advantage through designing quality multi-channel customer experiences with a greater emphasis on technology.

Innovations are often alike these days. Manufacturers use incremental innovations in products and then market these as new product variations. An example is the latest line extension from the Coco-Cola brand, Coke Life. Naturally sweetened and low calorie the Coke Life product story sounds very similar to the Pepsi Max promise.

Then, once in a while, a new market (with a new type of customer) is created for an innovation that disrupts the status quo and displaces existing technology. An example of this is the ultra-efficient Toyota Prius, a hybrid motor vehicle that is widely used as an example of disruptive innovation. When car manufacturer Toyota released the car in 1997 it was the first mass-produced hybrid vehicle and its appeal was niche. Today, the Prius range has global appeal, with 4.8 million cars sold and 67.7% market share of 7 million hybrids sold to date.[57]

The rapid pace of change is seeing personal technology evolve from a utility – helping with everyday productivity – to a life-enhancing tool that connects and enables interaction with the world around us. Innovation is set to intensify, as smart, connected products emerge, triggering more innovation, higher productivity, improved economic growth and a new era of competition – innovations such as: smart keys that open doors remotely, mirrors that can analyse your health, driverless cars, drones, 3D printing, and MEM (micro-electro-mechanical) technology that's being included in products such as smart fabric that can

---

57   Wikipedia, Toyota Prius

monitor the wearer's temperature, heart rate and location. For brands to succeed in this era, they will need to be in sync with their customers' behaviours and preferences; they will need to be agile and adaptable.

Out with the old

Creating great customer experiences at every touchpoint in the customer journey can easily unravel when customer/brand interactions are hampered by legacy technologies. Some company systems date back 10 to 20 years, stifling customer experience initiatives from a lack of access to data, integration, performance and resource availability.

Legacy systems can create a fragmented view of customer interactions making it impossible to translate customer data into actionable insights. For example, a segment of customers might be very active in the social space and therefore prefer their customer service interactions through social media instead of email communications. Older Content Management Systems (CMS) would be unable to provide this data quality, making customer personalisation unfeasible.

Marketing effort has been focused on web experiences for the past decade and innovation in CMS now provides not only content and interactivity but also analytics for marketing. Organisations now have the ability to collect data from the first web visit through to purchasing. This information can then be collected in a single database and integrated into a Customer Relationship Management

(CRM) system, bridging organisational silos through a single customer view and delivering higher engagement through targeted, automated and personalised experiences throughout the customer life cycle.

Big data

From digital channels comes a vast quantity of consumer information that is framed as one of marketing's most used buzzwords, 'big data'. Data-driven marketing has transformed the customer experience, enabling more effective engagement at every touchpoint in the customer journey. Most notable is e-commerce retailer Amazon's recommendation algorithm, which delivers customer recommendations and personalisation, Pandora's personally curated radio and beauty retailer Sephora's interactive physical and digital shopping experiences.

Physical retail environments are set to be transformed through the use of beacons. Beacons use BLE (Bluetooth Low Energy) technology and will enable retail, banking, transport and healthcare sectors greater engagement with customers through their mobile devices. When customers are within the vicinity of a beacon it connects with the customer's smartphone and captures contextual data that enables optimisation experiences such as personalisation. Technology companies such as Nike+ Fuelband, Fitbit and Jawbone have already implemented BLE technology to enable wearers access to personal information on their health and wellness on their smart devices.

These brands are in no doubt about the power and value that comes from customer behavioural data and wearable computing. The technology is touted as the next big opportunity for marketers to develop digital and real-world experiences. This year, Disney introduced their new customer management system called MyMagic+. According to the *New York Times*, the initiative, which will enhance the Disney experience, is set to build both loyalty and sales, through happier guests spending more money.[58] The initiative is costing Disney between $800 million and a billion dollars.

MyMagic+ collects personal data using wearable technology called MagicBand. The band links to an individual's profile and is used to collect vast amounts of customer intelligence and personalise the guest experience. Guests wearing the MagicBand have cashless access to ticketing, turnstile entrance, advance ride bookings, merchandise, food and beverage, customer service and VIP events; the list goes on. 'Disney extracts and integrates all the information about the guest from all the park siloed data systems as well as external sources. This allows them to create a longitudinal view of each guest's behaviour over channels, activities and time.'[59]

Based on this data, Disney can map the entire customer journey through each touchpoint, measuring the level of

58   Brook Barnes, 'At Disney Parks, A Bracelet Meant to Build Loyalty (And Sales)', *New York Times*, 7 January 2013

59   Ravi Kalakota, 'Guest Personalization and Wearable Computing: Disney My Magic+', *Business Analyst* 3.0, 10 March 2014

engagement with products, rides and characters, including what they ate and drank. Did the customer buy a balloon? Did she shake Mickey Mouse's hand but not Goofy's? This is what ultra-personalisation is set to look like; contextually predictive analytics that enable, for example, the customer's favourite character, Mickey Mouse, to surprise and delight by greeting the guest by name.

Predictive analytics

Predictive analytics (snippets of information to form a prediction) is also being used in emerging technologies to create proactive experiences. *Forbes* describes a proactive customer experience as, 'controlling the situation by causing action rather than waiting to respond to an event'.[60] A 'situation' could be the frustration of having an airline flight cancelled at the last minute. The approach to this situation could be: the airline would send notification that the flight has been cancelled and, anticipating their customers' needs, provide passengers with a list of next available flights for priority booking.

Customer care and support that is moving from reactive to proactive communication is the type of customer experience thinking that drives engagement and satisfaction. Delta Airline's smartphone, tablet and mobile-friendly website has the capabilities to keep their customers up to date while they're on the move. The airline updates

---

60   John Goodman, 'How To Create A Proactive Customer Experience',
      Forbes, 9 April 2014

passengers regarding delays, cancellations and changes in weather at their destination. The airline's suite of mobile device apps delivers notifications, allowing their customers to re-book in real-time. This proactive approach has led to reduced call volumes and fewer negative social media interactions.

These types of proactive experiences are emerging in 'personal assistant' apps too. Google has released Google Now, the next generation of apps that use predictive analytics. These apps make personalised recommendations by learning users' routines, using data stored in online searches, location data, emails, calendars, address books, social media and other contextual information. Technically Google Now can anticipate what the user will do next without being asked. For example, if your online calendar receives a meeting invite, Google Now will create a reminder, update the meeting invite with directions and calculate the commute.

Next generation apps

According to Forrester, the next apps will be developed for specific roles, processes and personas. 'Predictive algorithms will optimise around the patterns of similar individuals or behaviour.'[61] These next generation apps will be developed especially for different business functions such as marketing, sales or expense management. Individuals

---

61   Michael Yamnitsky, 'Three Proactive Assistant Startups Worth Watching', Forrester, 19 December 2013

in the workplace, customers and suppliers will increasingly rely on smart apps that anticipate and proactively help individuals connect and interact.

As characterised by an era of rapid change, organisations that wish to remain competitive will need to engineer enterprising innovation agendas with a customer-centric approach. This approach, when applied to creating great customer experiences that are seamless and deliver shared value, will provide organisations with a platform for the growth of their brands.

13

Pillar Six:
Co-creation

Traditionally, brands have kept innovation in product and service development in-house. However, organisations wanting rethinking innovation to boost their competitive edge have turned to customer groups, communities and start-ups to participate in crowdsourced intelligence. Driven by the proliferation of smartphones, the emergence of the super-connected consumer and positive contributions to corporate social responsibility, there has been increased adoption of crowd-driven innovation over the last 10 years. This is the process of creating products, services and experiences in collaboration with brand stakeholders in exchange for a voice in what gets developed, designed and manufactured; the process ultimately delivering shared value. The power of co-creation is the way it assists brands to think more broadly about their customer and their environments, helping brands see clearly from multiple perspectives.

Crowd-driven or *co-creation* innovation design can be applied to any sized problem or opportunity and is essentially generating value from open innovation.

Brand leaders are leveraging the creative power of co-creation design, although some are classed more as marketing initiatives or sales promotions, where communities of customers participate without contributing to the innovation process. An example is Pepsi's Refresh Project, which leveraged the power of the voting community to award $20 million in grants for ideas that will have a positive impact on the community.[62] Other brands, such as Procter & Gamble with their Connect and Develop program, are the pioneers of open innovation and have committed to acquiring up to 50% of their innovations from outside their organisation.[63]

Joint creation

For the tech-savvy Millennial who values participation and collaboration with brands and instant gratification through their experiences, co-creation is a high-involvement innovation process that delivers deep engagement and emotionally rich experiences.

The influence of co-creation participation on brand experience is customer value created by stimulating higher engagement and driving advocacy. In the white paper

62   Wikipedia, Pepsi Refresh Project

63   Larry Huston and Nabil Sakkab, 'Connect and Develop: Inside Procter & Gamble's New Model for Innovation', *Harvard Business Review*, 2006

'Influences of Co-creation on Experience', author Herbjorn Hysveen's study showed that 'customers creation with a brand – stimulating their engagement with the brand – influences brand experience, and through that, brand satisfaction and loyalty'. Hysveen goes on to say 'co-creation participation positively influences sensory, affective, cognitive, behavioural and rational dimensions of a brand experience'.[64]

International brand Marriott Hotels has 500 hotels in 60 countries and has set about collaborating with their customers to assist the brand in rethinking the future of travel. Marriott shifted the process of product and service design from a traditional approach to inviting guests, aficionados, influencers and experts to engage and contribute their ideas in revitalising the brand's travel experience. Using digital and social platforms, customer groups and likeminded enthusiasts participated in the community to cultivate conversations to co-create new guest experiences in design, technology, menus and wellness. Forging deeper connections with the next generation of travellers, who effortlessly fuse work and play, is at the heart of Marriott's 'Travel Brilliantly' strategy.[65]

64   Herbjørn Nysveen, 'Influences of Co-Creation on Brand Experience: The Role of Brand Engagement', WARC, 2014

65   Travel Brilliantly, Marriott Hotels, Corporate Website

Unified by the brand

A customer experience strategy that's increasingly being used by organisations to foster deeper brand engagement and personalised connection with customers is crowd-sourcing and collaboration through brand communities. A brand community is a group of customers who share a common interest and are unified by the brand. At the community's heart is a product or service, and it is the community members, in collaboration with the brand, that define the community's culture, beliefs and conduct, and brand-related activities. Bringing customers together with the same experiences develops a deep sense of community, galvanising the brand's promise and shared value.

Creating a community enables a brand to tap into collective insight and the shared experience of people outside the organisation. People participate for many reasons: to be emotionally connected to likeminded people, to indulge a shared passion or interest, or to contribute to the greater good. My agency helped revitalise the famous legwear brand Razzamatazz by introducing the brand to the next generation of stocking wearers, helping younger lovers of fashion to connect and share their fashion stories. A social community was established online based on an interactive fashion 'look book', called 'Next Girl'. Members of the community could create a stocking fashion look, take a photo, tag it with a description – for example, 'Lovely Legs 11' – then post their look online to the campaign microsite. The online community created thousands of online conversations and social interactions with very high engagement. What we didn't expect was the level of passion and the extraordinary lengths community members went to in creating each of their fashion looks.

Communities such as these enable brands to collaborate with their current and potential customers in value creation and provide a platform for people to engage with and advocate the brand. Importantly, it gives loyal customers a space to share their brand love. Successful brand communities are built on allowing group members to influence relationships and shape behavioural norms. This was most evident when one member decided to get naughty with inappropriate fashion looks that revealed more skin than stocking. Within the group the opinion leaders voiced their concerns, and the community rallied behind their sentiments in calling for the offending images to be removed.

Brand crowdsourcing

Brand crowdsourcing or co-creation strategy is the practice of engaging people from across the customer experience ecosystem to seek knowledge, strategic insights, problem-solving solutions, innovation and design. The process has been used by a large number of organisations, including McDonald's, Samsung, Dell, Unilever and Oreo. Crowdsourcing is effective because it draws together a large group of high-value customers and brand loyalists with diverse, mass intelligence and the potential to solve business challenges of all kinds.

Lego is a brand that has been crowdsourcing new product design since 2008. The organisation's objective is to increase the number of product ideas while improving customer engagement. Lego has 180 designers working on product ideas and crowdsourcing helps with this process. Using Lego assets, fans submit their designs to the website Lego Ideas. The more fans participate in the community – that is, the more fans support, share and create – the more 'clutch power' points are received in the form of points and gadgets.

When a fan submits their idea for a new product the community votes, and when a submission reaches 10,000 votes, Lego evaluates and selects which designs get developed. Fans whose ideas are selected receive a 1% royalty on the net revenue and designer credit in the set material. Winners have included a miniature version of NASA's Mars Rover Curiosity, created by a NASA engineer, and the Ghostbusters Lego set created by a 35-year-old Australian fan.

For Lego the strategy of crowdsourcing product design delivers an extremely cost effective new product development channel, with unsuccessful ideas costing nothing and projects that are successful costing the company a modest royalty. Marketing of new products also benefits, with fans in the community selecting what's hot and what's not. For example, the Lego set based on Minecraft received

10,000 votes in two days. For Lego, brand crowdsourcing is delivering clear insight on what the customer wants to see in-market and pre-launch buzz that only a substantial marketing investment could buy.

Experience design

Despite the latest Forrester research which shows that 50% of organisations in Australia rate customer experience as one of their top strategic priorities, very few businesses involve customers in the customer experience design process.[66] Experience design is a framework for innovation using research to identify physical and digital touchpoints of engagement. Of importance in experience design is a customer-centric approach and the inclusion of both customers and employees in the co-creation process to deliver shared value. This helps to humanise the design process with richer insights that are more relevant. For today's brands in the experience economy, co-creation needs to be part of the marketer's toolbox. Customer group participation creates engagement and redefines the customer relationship, adding different perspectives and enriching the process of experience design.

---

66   Nadia Cameron, 'Aussie Organisations Not Transforming Enough for
     Customer Experience Excellence: Forrester', COM.com, 13 August 2014

14

Pillar Seven: Experience Management

There's no escaping the fact: brands today need to be data-driven and measurability for marketers is an imperative. Whether it's the brand's market share, brand preference, marketing return on investment, customer acquisition, customer behaviour, web analytics or social engagement, managing brand performance improves the effectiveness of marketing through better understanding of the customers' needs.

With top-performing businesses moving their brand focus to customer experience, greater importance is now being placed on measuring the customer/brand relationship; that is, the total customer experience. Measuring customer satisfaction and advocacy provides brands with customer relationship understanding, insights into purchasing behaviour, growth of customer recommendations, and improved business performance into the future.

Net Promoter Score

Used as a leading indicator of brand health, Net Promoter Score (NPS) is the industry's global standard for measuring customer experience. NPS measures future performance by asking one question: whether a customer would recommend a brand, product or service to a friend or colleague. With top-performing brands treating customer advocacy as a future driver of business revenue, NPS's measure of customer advocacy, when combined with business financial metrics, provides a forward view of the health of the brand.

What makes NPS attractive to businesses is the measurement is easily understood by all company stakeholders and is easily disseminated across the wider business. NPS features three segments: Promoters (loyal enthusiasts), Passives (satisfied but unenthusiastic) and Detractors (unhappy customers). The concept behind the measurement is to create more loyal customers (Promoters) that advocate the brand and to reduce the numbers of Detractors to achieve a higher score. NPS is a metric that best measures total customer experience – that is, all customer touchpoints in the customer journey – rather than a single brand/customer interaction. For example, if a business was to measure customer service that resulted in a low NPS, the dissatisfaction could be attributed to the customer service or the product offering. The business in this case would be better served to measure satisfaction of the call centre (a single brand/customer interaction) and include the NPS measure in a broader context.

Leading metric

As a measure of future financial performance, NPS – when combined with financial metrics – delivers a forward measure of business health and an understanding of how customer experience impacts Customer Lifetime Value (CLV) (a prediction of the customer's profitability over the lifetime of the relationship[67]). Often a light goes on when NPS is explained to businesses in the context of retention and acquisition. Traditionally, much of marketing's effort has been focused on acquiring new customers at the expense of existing customers. In the meantime, unhappy customers – the NPS segment called Detractors – are brand switching, and even worse, telling their friends and peers about their new brand experience. What's emerged from Bain and Company's Net Promoter System global NPS benchmarking research is that brands with higher NPS scores than their competitors – that is, their customers are engaged, satisfied and promoting the brand – have growth rates two times higher than those with average NPS scores.[68]

---

67 Wikipedia, Customer Lifetime Value

68 Net Promoter Score and System, The Net Promoter Community, Corporate Website

Change for the better

For this reason, progressive organisations are taking NPS one step further and using the metric to embed continuous culture change and drive customer-centric behaviour as a whole-of-business approach. NIB Health Fund is one of the top four Australian health insurance brands. The business launched its program to implement a voice of the customer strategy using Net Promoter Score to significantly transform the brand operationally and culturally.

Prior to adopting NPS, the brand's biggest hurdle in delivering total customer experiences was the business. Marketing and distribution teams were working independently, and while customer retention was a company-wide agenda, no one was accepting responsibility for its underperformance.

Speaking at the Customer 360 Symposium, Head of Customer Experience, Adam Novak said, 'NPS is doing two things – it's creating an environment for zero tolerance of customer failure, and for delivering great customer service'.[69] NIB embarked on a three-stage program, and in doing so raised its NPS by 20 points. Firstly, data was collected on what customers thought of NIB's products and services – this led to the better soundproofing for their dental centres. NPS was then included in the brand's quarterly satisfaction survey – this led to a new website for

---

69 Nadia Cameron, 'How NPS Has Helped NIB Keep Customers', CMO.com, 31 March 2015

members to search and compare extras providers such as physiotherapists, chiropractors, orthodontists, etc.

From the NPS data the brand has identified that their Promoters have a much higher retention rate. One of the greatest learnings for Novak was the insights from their lowest scoring Detractors, and as a result the organisation calls all customers in this segment to get deeper understandings.

NIB people, processes and systems were then aligned. Action was required quickly or momentum would be lost. A 'quick wins forum' was established with six frontline representatives and six team leaders across product, digital and IT. To support the 'quick wins forum', NIB introduced a quality improvements team to analyse customer data for insights to improve the brand's offering. Two new dedicated teams managing customer plans and customer retention forged better relationships.

Another lever used to create culture shift was embedding NPS into all employee bonuses and KPIs, from the CEO to frontline staff. Novak said, 'NPS has made a significant and positive contribution to NIB – the cultural change required to transition to a customer-first business can't be underestimated'.[70]

70   Nadia Cameron, 'How NPS Has Helped NIB Keep Customers', CMO.com, 31 March 2015

Social listening

NPS is now a widely used metric for taking the temperature of customer satisfaction and advocacy, and in this ever-evolving market, brands need real-time measures of customer opinion too. Brands that measure NPS should also develop an ongoing listening program that integrates real-time customer experience monitoring into their business metrics. Effective customer experience management requires daily monitoring to understand what each NPS segment is saying about the brand and social listening enables marketers to hear how customers are talking about their brand experiences online. These are unprompted contextual conversations that provide insight into the customers' world and what's important to them; it gives access to conversations to help brands provide better engagement and interaction, which in turn builds stronger relationships. It is a valuable resource for identifying emerging popular culture trends and measuring brand and competitor share of voice.

Voice of the Customer

In the past, a Voice of the Customer (VoC) program meant a lot of different things to organisations: classic surveys, social media monitoring, speech analytics, web analytics. Today, there's a standardisation of the term, and if you're speaking to a colleague and they have a VoC program in place they are measuring cross-channel feedback.

In the experience economy the importance of under-standing customer needs, wants and pain points cannot be overestimated, and for this reason VoC programs now serve as the premium offering in customer experience manage-ment. VoC is a term that describes a closed-loop customer experience measurement that facilitates the delivery of better experiences. Programs consist of the analysis of cus-tomer data from Net Promoter Scores, cross-channel sur-veys, open text comments, qualitative research, employee insights on customer issues, online engagement data and social media feedback. These measures then provide data on drivers of engagement and satisfaction.

Breaking down the barriers

A critical consideration point for organisations is a cross-organisation view of the customer feedback. A common problem is that many businesses already capture cus-tomer feedback from single sources using technologies from a variety of vendors, and more often than not this valuable information never leaves a particular depart-ment. So while individual departments benefit, enabling that team to resolve narrow customer issues, a joined-up view of the customer experience would benefit the whole organisation.

Progressive brands are breaking down these organi-sational silos and integrating their customer data sets. While this sounds ideal on paper, combining different data feeds and data formats has many challenges and is not at all straightforward. One solution is through enterprise software such as a feedback management platform which manages customer feedback from different external and internal sources, and partnering with other vendors such as social listening platforms to provide reporting and action management.

Better customer feedback

In most cases an organisation's key touchpoints are well established before a VoC program is built. Multi-channel VoC programs can be greatly assisted through developing a clear understanding of Customer Purchase Journey Mapping. Mapping provides the business with the customer's point of view instead of an internal process perspective, and will show which brand/customer intersections are the most influential, those intersections that are customer pain points, and where the experience gaps lie. By understanding how the customer experiences the brand at these points a VoC program can monitor, measure and report on customer feedback.

What has become evident is the importance of timely collection of customer feedback. Information should be collected within hours of the experience to provide accuracy, and this is where the power of mobile is helping brands deliver real-time actionable insights. Gathering information on how customers experience the brand across different touchpoints has the direct effect of fine tuning the customer experience, and in doing so, increasing their level of engagement and satisfaction.

Important learning

While many brands have an insatiable appetite for big data, 'forty-five percent of companies have not established a mechanism for responding to either negative or positive customer feedback. These unresponsive brands ask customers to spend time giving feedback but aren't returning the favour, leaving problems unresolved and opportunities unrealised.'[71] Research company Forrester points to the lack of internal processes such as defining the right actions and prioritising the most important improvement projects as the hurdles that are preventing systematic improvements in customer experience.

Managing and evaluating customer experience is a business imperative. Marketers need actionable insights from different data sources to help their organisation better understand the connection between customer behaviour and the experience.

---

71   Maxie Schmidt-Subramanian with Harley Manning, Dylan Czarneck, 'The State of Voice of the Customer Programs, 2014: It's Time to Act', Forrester, 2014

Part Three

MARKETING THE EXPERIENCE

15

Mobile First

Today's reality is that we are constantly connected. The moment we wake we reach for the phone and we're connected, accessing information throughout the day and into the evening: the weather, bank balances, email, a quick social media status update, a search on wearable tech, shopping online for new shoes or a recipe for tonight's dinner party – fact or fiction: we check our phones on average 150 times a day and 40% of all shopping-related queries in Australia now come from mobiles.[72] Smartphones have enabled access to information anytime and anywhere; portable, interactive mobile has changed how people discover and connect with brands and how they're sharing their experiences.

Eighty one percent of Australians now own a smartphone, making this country one of the most digitally connected places on Earth.[73] Digital savvy and superconnected, we now have unprecedented access to anything

72   Mobile Trend Report, Research and Resources, IAB, 2013
73   Deloitte Mobile Customer Survey, 2014

and everything through thousands of media channels. This has fundamentally impacted traditional marketing communication and provided new opportunities for brands to connect and engage with their customers. More than ever, the mobile device is the mainspring of brand experience, connecting the empowered customers at every touchpoint along the purchase journey – from searching, to reviewing, to comparing prices, finding a store location and sharing user-generated content online.

Mobile mindset

For many marketers however this small and powerful piece of technology still lacks the importance to be considered more seriously than any other advertising channel. 'In fact, only 17 percent of marketers have mobile strategies that are fully integrated and aligned with their overarching marketing strategies while 31 percent admit that they either have no strategy or simply view mobile as a campaign and not a business strategy.'[74]

By using the platform for demand generation only, marketers are forgoing the unrealised opportunity of contextual engagement at every stage of the customer journey. Data collected from customer behaviour – such as location, time of day, purchase preferences, social influence and device types – is enabling sophisticated marketers to shape

74   'Getting In Sync With Mobile Customers', COM Council, 2014

engagement and create one-to-one, always-on, personalised experiences for their customers.

What's evident is that consumers are already mobile-first and brands need to be too. For this reason, brands need to evolve their marketing strategies to leverage broader customer engagement that reflects everyday, blended, digital and physical, search to social behaviours.

Device relevant

Customers' purchasing behaviour is now a non-linear path of online and offline interactions. Unlike yesterday's path-to-purchase, it doesn't start when the customer walks in-store and finish with the purchase – today's customer journey may start with brand discussions with friends over coffee, move to online customer word-of-mouth recommendations, and end with a purchase online. Or it could begin with a TV ad, move to researching various brand offers online, shift in-store to gather more information where the purchase takes place, and finish with a Facebook check-in to update friends.

At each stage of the customer purchase journey the mobile device is present and always on. For marketers this requires a shift in mindset to ensure that the brand experience on mobile is aligned with customer expectations and is personalised, contextual and device-relevant. Brands that are delivering these seamless interactions are the brands that have become part of our lives and we talk about positively and most often; for example, Amazon,

Pandora, Apple, ASOS, Nike, AMEX and Google. These are the brands creating experiences that deliver value, feel good and even provide wow for customers.

Brands that can deliver a seamless experience, where each touchpoint is connected across the total brand experience, provide value to customers by satisfying their needs; that is, they make searching information easy for the user through using a mobile-friendly site or app, WIFI is available in-store enabling customers to share their experiences, they provide digital and physical customer service options and personalised online shopping using predictive data.

US brand Home Depot's mobile-first strategy is the shape of tomorrow's customer experience. Their customers can browse their range, locations and opening times and also select how they want their order to be paid for and delivered. 'The app uses location and context to reduce the friction between the user opening the app and finding their desired experiences. The app has two modes: the Default Mode, which is the standard app experience, and In-Store Mode, which is switch-activated by the user to indicate they are in the store'.[75] The latter mode specially caters for the physical experience by giving the user access to store layout, specials, shopping and cart. Home Depot's research showed that customer behaviour was different in store when they were making purchasing decisions compared for example to the planning phase of their projects. When a customer is in in-store mode they can access information

75   Mike Schneider, 'Designing for Place at the Home Depot', *UX Magazine*, 6 January 2015

on stock availability and the location of stock by aisle and bay.

Think context, not device

A recent report from IAB Australia suggests marketers need to stop thinking about devices that people are using and start thinking about context. Context is location, time of day or week, what those people are doing, and how the brand wants that person to respond to the marketing message. 'A person with a smartphone, TV and a tablet is one person, not three; someone who uses a tablet doesn't change into a different person just because they sit down at a computer. It's become clear that the device is really a proxy for what really matters: reaching people in the right context with the right message.'[76]

TripAdvisor's mobile thinking is developing apps that are reliable, useful and easy to use for their customers, such as the feature called 'Point Me There' to help the user know in which direction to walk. Head of mobile partnerships for TripAdvisor commented that, 'You really want people to come back to your app, so you have to ensure a seamless experience that provides real value for the customer...It's difficult to browse multiple sites on mobile.'[77] This has led the brand to develop a whole meta-search engine where customers read reviews, check ratings, and view photos and prices in a single window. This is a customer-centric

76   Mobile Trend Report, Research and Resources, IAB, 2013
77   'Getting In Sync With Mobile Customers', COM Council, 2014

mobile mindset which, combined with the circumvention of high roaming charges by enabling downloads of information onto user smart devices, alleviates a most often discussed travellers' pain point and creates a great customer experience.

Wearables

Wearable tech has gone mainstream, giving wearers access to bite-sized pieces of information called 'data snacking'. The apps on our mobile devices are set to get smarter, offering universal control of our appliances at home and a hub for our personal health data, and will be designed to provide personalised recommendations based on past behaviours.

Tech savvy marketers at the top end of town are keeping a close eye on the Apple Watch, with a keen interest in the apps that are being built for the platform. Instagram for example has developed a full browsing feed experience on the user's wrist. Wearers can also book an Uber car from the device with confirmation via picture of the car and plate number. With a bigger drive to use the Internet of Things (access to appliances and household functions through the internet) the Watch purports to enable users to check the status of their appliances, security, etc. at a glance – although our appliance manufactures have a little catching up to do!

For the very first time, Apple launched its new Watch product line through their physical stores for fans to interact with the device. Their point of view on the launch was that fans needed the opportunity to experience the device and select a style that's right for them before purchasing. While the move away from e-commerce was unexpected, it demonstrates the brand's appetite for creating physical experiences, especially in-store.

Geo-targeting

At present in Australia there are a number of corporate brands such as Woolworths, St George Bank and the Chatswood Chase Shopping Centre in Sydney that are experimenting with geolocation technology. The technology uses low-power, low-cost Bluetooth transmitters that detect a smart phone app when the user is within a certain distance of a beacon. World Cup sponsor Coca-Cola used the technology at the event to cut through the brand noise and bring their message to life when Cup visitors were in different areas of the stadium.

The beacon technology enables brands to personalise messages such as welcome to store, promotional offers, waiting times at checkouts, store layouts, and delivery of specific product information that's relevant and real-time. In addition to enhancing the customer experience, data collected provides rich customer insights into behaviour that will shape future physical and digital experiences.

Another location-based technology that's set to change personalisation is geo-fencing. Beacons and geo-fencing both identify a user's proximity to a location. The latter technology uses GPS coordinates and the mobile phone's location to pick up signals from the satellite network, enabling opt-in access to location-specific content such as a free offer. An example of this technology is Intel's plan to release a smartwatch, designed for parents to keep track of their children travelling to and from school.

Mobile ready

In less than 10 short years smart devices have shifted the brand/customer relationship. Mobile is now essential in connecting brands with their customers and bridging the gap between the customer's digital and physical worlds. Customers today see their mobile phone as an extension of the shopping experience and a connection between what's experienced physically and access to more information online, such as product/service searches, researching, finding a store location, price comparison or giving recommendations to their social networks.

At home or on the go, at anytime and anywhere customers are expecting a seamless experience at every touchpoint. People are already mobile 'ready to go' and brands today need to be mobile ready too – from being found in Google searches to optimising web and landing pages for mobile users. Smart marketers are now ensuring the customer experience is end to end with sophisticated smart device apps that personalise the individual's experience.

16

Making it Personal

We've become accustomed to personalised digital experiences, so much so they're expected in our daily interactions with brands. Personalisation is the idea that the products and services we interact with should be relevant and tailored to individual preferences, behaviour and context. Data, combined with powerful recommendation and automation technology, now delivers high-speed, personalised experiences for movies, music, shopping and social media on any device, anywhere and at any time, helping brands create deep connections along the customer journey.

For many marketers, personalisation ranks as a top commercial priority, and no wonder, with research from the Econsultancy 2015 Digital Trends Report showing that, on average, brands that are personalising the customer experience are reporting a 14% uplift in sales.[78] However, personalisation is still on a low-level scale, and many brands are only utilising personalisation for

---

78   2015 Digital Trend report, Econsultancy, 2015

marketing communications such as emails, online advertising and smart apps. As barriers to entry are reduced – thereby providing access to cost-effective personalisation technology – this will enable businesses to achieve the sort of competitive advantage the pioneers in this space are delivering.

Best in market

Personalisation of customer experiences enables deeper engagement and the creation of stronger brand relationships that endure over time. Amazon, Google, Apple and Pandora are the pioneers of personalisation, collecting every click, swipe, post and purchase to improve engagement. These are the brands that know where we live and what language we speak, they know the time of day we interact, they know our personal preferences based on the purchases we've made, and they can anticipate what we might like next.

While radio has been in our homes since the late 19th century it only took Pandora Radio 10 years to disrupt the traditional market, offering listeners personalised selections based on a music genome that identifies over 400 musical attributes in a song and then plays another song that has the same traits.

Amazon too creates personalised experiences with a one-to-one friendly greeting at the top of the customer's homepage, along with requests to review products, product recommendations based on browsing and purchasing history, email updates and social integration. Couple this with low-priced shopping and fast shipping and shopping online with Amazon is an experience that feels like 'they just get me'.

Humanising the connection between the brand and the customer through personalisation creates more meaningful experiences that lead to deeper customer relationships. Beverage manufacturer Coca-Cola's personalisation strategy saw the brand personalise cans and bottles of Coke with 250 popular names in the company's 'Share a Coke' campaign. In doing so, Coke reversed years of sales decline on the back of one of the most talked about and shared campaigns of recent times.

Shop 'til you drop

In the current era it is critical to design personalised interactions that seamlessly move the audience between physical and digital experiences and across their personal devices. Wanting to disrupt the traditional clothing store fitting-room experience, A&G Labs in Philadelphia set about designing a super-connected 'three screen' fitting-room to create a stronger customer path-to-purchase.[79]

A&G Labs' own research showed that shoppers were 71% more likely to purchase when they tried on a garment, whereas the online shopping experience delivered the opportunity for shoppers to search, read customer

---

79   Sharon Pathak, 'Fitting Room 2.0: A Three-Screen Experience to Help You Try on Jeans', Digiday, 13 August 2014

reviews, compare prices and to 'share' their purchases. A&G Labs' 'three-screen' design merges a touchscreen in the store fitting-room with a customer's smartphone and a tablet used by the store assistant.

The customer begins the journey by signing into a smart app and scanning a barcode with their phone to link their device to the screen in the fitting-room. Garments that are taken into the fitting-room are scanned using the swing-tag barcodes and appear on the fitting-room touch-screen, enabling customers to find out more information on the article of clothing, see alternative styles and recom-mended accessories, read online reviews, and 'ask for help' via the sales assistant's tablet. Each step of the customer journey is monitored on the tablet by the sales assistant, enabling a personalised experience. When the customer finds the perfect garment they can share the find with their peers via social media, earning a discount that is then saved to their smartphone app, ready to claim at check-out.

Making it easy

Social login is an alternative method for signing into a third-party website using information from a customer's social networking site such as Facebook, Twitter or Google+. It is used to simplify customer logins by replacing the customer registration process of creating a login and password which they then have to recall. The benefit for brands is through the acquisition of rich customer intel-ligence. This type of registration helps brands personalise the customer's online experience based on their social behaviour by utilising user data that brands simply could not ask for at registration stage.

Take Facebook's registration process to become a member: fans provide demographic information such as date of birth, gender, relationship status, career, and email address for verification. Layer this with psychographic information such as human interest – movies, music, hobbies, religious and political persuasions – and add 'likes' from web browsing via the user's Facebook profile and brands have access to a lot of rich information that's most often accurate and current.

Marketers are beginning to access richer social media and smart app data – including sentiment, contextual behaviour and emotional states – to deliver sophisticated multi-channel personalisation. US retailer Walmart uses social login with their Facebook application called 'Shopycat'. The gift-giving app uses Social Genome technology to analyse Facebook friend likes, shares and posts, and then matches their interests to an extensive catalogue of products from Walmart.com.

Developed by WalmartLabs, Social Genome is Walmart's giant database that captures public, private and social data such as tweets, Facebook posts, blogs and videos, and mines this data to target products based on a customer's genome.

Creating meaningful and personalised customer experiences is the new currency of marketing. As we continue to race into a new era of relationship marketing where personalisation has become an everyday expectation, brands need deep customer insights from behaviour and deep understanding of customer/brand interactions to provide emotionally positive experiences along the purchase journey. Marketers will deliver this new order using enterprise software vendors, data analytics and digital developers to deliver the right personalised experiences at the right time.

A little creepy

Increasingly, more people are willing to share their personal information in exchange for higher quality experiences such as ease of logon, access to knowledgeable customer service, previous purchase and browsing history, and relevant branded content. The challenge for marketers going forward is how to improve the customer experience without being perceived as intrusive or even creepy.

To create unique experiences brands need to understand as much as possible about the purchaser. Conversely, one of the big concerns around this topic is privacy. As people become more personal data literate, organisations will need to evolve their data management practices and demonstrate transparency in data collection: how the data will be used, permissions around sharing data, and enabling users to opt in and out of targeting. Given the amount of data that is required to be collected to create personalised recommendations, brands need to demonstrate effective use and ethical behaviour in order not to erode the trust that is intrinsic in their relationship with their customers.

Privacy has become a near universal concern, with people questioning how their data is being used and consumers becoming acutely aware that brands are capturing personal information for marketing purposes – so much so that there are privacy-enhancing platforms and tools that enhance customers' privacy protection by identifying which companies are tracking them and assisting in blocking them.

Consumer concerns are reflected in research from the US that indicates that 92% of online users are worried about their privacy; 86% of users take steps to protect their privacy; and 86% would use a Do Not Track button if this feature was available.[80] However, from Facebook's Mark Zuckerberg's perspective, we're in a post-privacy era, with Zuckerberg announcing in 2010 that 'privacy is dead', though now it seems that privacy is back on Facebook's agenda, no longer a social norm but as a business model.[81] It would seem people are becoming more comfortable sharing their personal information as long as it's for a fair exchange, such as better online experiences.

While there's truth in Zuckerberg's comment, his point of view doesn't reflect why Snapchat-style apps seem to be so much in favour with Millennials. According to my teen daughter and her friends, they use the platform because their texts and pictures are posted and then within a

80   TRUSTe, Gallup, Accenture, 2014
81   Will Oremus, 'Facebook's Privacy Pivot', *Slate*, 25 July 2014

couple seconds all trace of the post is gone. A privacy study in 2014 found that, 'Millennials are redefining privacy as a fair value exchange and are wary of brands that abuse this exchange'.[82] What has become apparent is the under 35s are increasingly prepared to switch products or services because of privacy concerns.

As we move forward to a time of greater transparency, brands will need to encourage individuals to share their personal information by helping them to understand how it's being used. This will result in customers sharing better quality data in return for saving time and money; just one example of personalisation and experiences that make life easier and more rewarding.

---

82   'Privacy In Perspective (And Numbers)', Contagious, 12 May 2014

17

Brands as Publishers

Content marketing has undergone a seismic shift from traditional, keyword-heavy website content to content that's relevant, meaningful, engaging and entertaining in various formats, from 140 characters, to six-second videos, to long-form content that matches the form and function of the platform in which it appears and – most of all – to content that delivers value. More importantly, organisations are moving into the less familiar role of 'brands as content publishers', leveraging social channels, paid search, native advertising and paid distribution platforms to build their own audiences.

Content is king

In essence, content marketing is the art of creating, curating and amplifying content combined with the science of measuring its impact on awareness, engagement, acquisition and customer satisfaction. In the era of all things digital and social, people's newsfeeds – rather than publisher's content and brand pages – have become the conduit through which content is liked and shared. These days, because engagement leads to reach, most brands seed their content with a media spend in order to ignite a social response; in many cases the like, the share and the comment are how success is measured.

The exponential growth in content marketing is being driven by brands shifting from push to pull marketing. This shift is being driven by changes in audience engagement with brands. Social channels are providing brands the opportunity to cost-effectively reach large audience numbers at a lower media cost, and the convergence of paid, earned and owned media is making it more difficult to distinguish brand messages from media-published content.

Distribution is queen

Many marketers have spent recent years building their social communities, and while a large number of brand communities have grown exponentially, marketers are still not leveraging their communities as effective distribution channels. It would seem that lightweight, re-shared entertainment and link or click bait – with low to no investment in content production – is ticking the social box with brands. The development of creative brand assets which deliver the brand promise, are highly visual and communicate the brand story provide an authentic voice that deepens engagement with the audience.

What's on the agenda of many marketers is how to lift the performance of their content marketing campaigns. There are two schools of thought here – quantity v quality – and neither approach is a guarantee of results or a determinant of how much time and money should be spent on distribution. One thing for certain is that publishing great content gets it shared through people's social ecosystems and utilising paid distribution delivers audience reach. The fact remains that content without an effective media distribution strategy will never convert into anything more for the brand than a small number of likes and shares. Great content that resides on a brand website or blog, waiting to be discovered, with the assumption that it will attract an audience with an upload to YouTube, a Facebook post feeding from Instagram and a few tweets, is a guarantee of poor content marketing ROI.

Contemporary marketers are ensuring audiences can easily discover and engage with content in their preferred online environment that is not necessarily a brand-led platform. This social distribution strategy moves the discovery of content from the audience searching for your brand, product or service to the audience engaging through interesting and/or entertaining opportunities, such as paid brand/publisher content (native advertising), earned media (PR-led editorial), event and media partnerships (Super Bowl), breaking the news or leveraging cultural trends (brand newsroom), AdWords and re-marketing gated reports and white papers. These are just a handful of examples of how to reach to a wider audience using paid content to deliver an improved ROI for the marketing effort.

The convergence of news

Today, many people are getting their daily news and updates from their social media newsfeed. Traditional media content segmentation has been disrupted; standalone news, sports, business and social content have all but disappeared online. Now, all types of content forms are clumped together. Think of the average person's Facebook newsfeed where you'll find social events, kids' weekend sports, news on terrorist attacks, pictures of cats, posts about political issues and much more. Smart devices have shifted how people use media, and for advertisers the native format delivers an in-stream, non-intrusive, platform-relevant brand message.

Innovative marketers are becoming increasingly sophisticated content producers, and with this comes the next trend: to evolve this model and become content publishers. Marketers will need to think and act like editors and journalists with a broadcast agenda. Their teams will develop, create and distribute sound bites, video, text, pictures, blogs and digital assets, and feed it to their websites, social media sites and traditional media outlets using paid and earned channels.

There has also been a number of corporate brands entering the emerging world of brand journalism and establishing brand newsrooms. A brand newsroom is where an organisation drives the publishing of content that's real-time, follows conversation trends, produces content around these trends and in some cases breaks and makes the news stories. It's content that adheres to the brand narrative and articulates the brand story. The stories created have a journalistic mindset, building a relationship with the reader and finding stories that are contextually relevant and add value to the audience experience.

An internal brand newsroom needs to have capacity and speed, and can be resource-heavy with creatives, writers, producers, videographers, designers, production, social media staff and data analysts. The people best suited to lead these teams are those with a blend of marketing and publishing expertise working in combination.

Playing the advantage

The Australian Football League (AFL) launched its fully-fledged brand newsroom, staffed and resourced to provide content, with the objective of establishing a credible news organisation. Head of Content at AFL Media Matt Pinkney believes that the content function is to protect the brand, promote AFL into expanding markets, get more Australians involved in the sport and promote membership. A former Walkley-award winning News Ltd journalist with the *Herald Sun* in Melbourne, Pinkney doesn't see the content that AFL Media produces as content marketing, instead it's content journalism. Under his watch, the content that's produced needs to be credible and trustworthy. The relationship with the audience needs to be built on trust through transparent and objective editorial.

Spurred on by the success of US Major League Baseball's newsroom, the *Global Mail* reported that the AFL injected a $5 million investment into AFL Media. Bringing the Australian Rules coverage back in-house has posed a threat to rival mainstream publishers News Ltd and Fairfax Media, who question AFL Media's independent coverage of the game. At the same time AFL Media was growing its audience, News Ltd put its football coverage behind a paywall; the move turned away the *Herald Sun's* AFL audience in droves.

A new business model that operates on 100%-owned media has been created around bringing back the control of the content. AFL Media now employs over 110 people across an online and offline consumer publishing arm; a business-to-business division offering web development, design and photography services, and a video and stills production studio that produces content for its own media use, as well as clients Cricket Australia, Racing Australia and the AFL's corporate sponsors.[83]

At the end of the day, people want brands to act less like advertisers and act more like publishers. It becomes the responsibility of marketers to bring a high level of objectivity to their content marketing by building credibility and trust so audiences don't feel that it's just an opportunity for a quick sale.

---

83   Andrea Sophocleous, 'Brands Become Content Producers: Insights from Telstra, Samsung and AFL Media on Content Marketing', WARC, August 2013

18

When Art
Meets Science

Whether you're selling beverages, banks or beachfront apartments, the daily challenge that all marketers face is how to connect, engage and build worlds that customers want to be part of. While there's no definitive answer, what's relevant in the experience economy is an idea that tells a story, which is then enabled by technology. It is the combination of a great idea, science and technology that's enabling brands to personalise experiences and build deeper connections with their customers, to deliver the moments-of-truth where their audience chooses one brand over the next.

There is no doubt that data and technology are the two tools that are driving results. Data helps to shape strategy by turning data sets into insights that direct thinking towards a great idea. However, data and technology aren't replacements for ideas that touch and connect with the audience.

Winning experience

This signals how creativity and technology both have a role to play in the digital era, and what matters is how the idea touches the audience because that's what starts a conversation and gets people actively participating in the brand story, rather than just receiving it. An example (and Cannes winner) of a great idea/science/technology combination was the British Airways (BA) campaign 'The Magic of Flying', created by UK agency OgilvyOne.

In an industry that's dominated by price discounting, the BA campaign celebrates the joy of flying with the idea that through a child's eyes there's something magical about large flying objects; we can't help but look up in wonder. The brief was to highlight the breadth of BA destinations, and this is where the idea was supercharged by technology and connected with people at scale.

Digital billboards used ADS-B antennas on nearby buildings and custom-built surveillance technology to collect live data from each aircraft's transponder. The data was then sent to a purpose-built dashboard, and as BA flights flew overhead the billboards updated the dynamic messaging in real-time with the plane's flight number and route.

The BA billboards could be found in Piccadilly, Central London and Chiswick, and created a special moment between the people watching and the planes flying overhead. This was an engaging idea that reminded us how magical flying is, and this simple idea got over 350 million people talking about the experience. The campaign increased traffic to the BA website by 75,000 unique visits and received 1 million YouTube views.[84]

Make it relevant

What we tend to forget as marketers is the audience viewing the campaign doesn't care about whether the creative has an emotional connection, whether the idea is fresh, innovative and entertaining, or if the messaging is 'on brand'. What they care about is what's in it for me; does the product say something about my life; will it make my life richer; how is it relevant to me? In a multiscreen world, audience attention is in short supply. To get attention brands need to be part of the cultural context and even need to challenge social convention. This requires content and experiences that compete with the rich experiences from publishers, celebrities, entertainment channels, gaming and social media – all vying for the same attention. It is the creative idea (and how it's executed) that will interrupt, connect and engage – changing the ordinary to the awesome.

---

84   Rae Ann Fera, 'Anatomy of a Cannes Contender: British
      Airways' Magic Posters That Point at Planes', Fast Company, 16 June 2014

19

Paid Media

Today people are bombarded with brand choices, audiences are inundated with marketing messages, consumers are super-connected and digitally empowered, and marketers face channel proliferation. This is a time when the currency of marketing has fundamentally and rapidly shifted to personalised, on-demand, seamless brand experiences across devices and channels.

The explosion of paid, earned and owned media channels is influencing how media is consumed, and that's driving how media is planned and creative advertising is activated. In the past few years alone, desktop has spilt into tablet, mobile, native app, smart TV, social and push messaging, making the task of reaching audiences a complex science. Media planning is now dependent on technology, machine learning and optimisation, with a greater need for media planners to quickly understand audience behavioural shifts and emerging platforms.

Going native

Native advertising is the term for branded content within an editorial context, and in many ways native ads do what display ads are trying to do – engage. Native is an emerging advertising format that integrates content marketing using the voice of the publisher to drive high cut through for advertisers.

Native ads appear within the stories of the site/publication and are non-intrusive, the ads looking and feeling like a publisher's content. Whereas traditional advertising serves to disrupt the user experience, native ads are highly relevant to the surrounding content, delivered as part of the reader experience, and are sharable across social channels.

Internet news media company BuzzFeed provides an enormous variety of content on topics from politics to amusing animal quizzes. The site has a massive audience of '150 million unique users helping sponsored content go viral every month. BuzzFeed's native ads look just like the rest of the whimsical posts made by the site every day, but with a small note at the top letting readers know it's been paid for by a brand and is not endorsed by the publication's editorial team.'[85]

As the native format matures, marketers will rely on their evolved internal marketing teams and their communication agencies to assist them in delivering real-time, third-party publisher content that has greater depth, context

85   'Trends Snapshot: The Future of Native Advertising', WARC, December 2013

and brand narrative. However, there are several challenges facing marketers, and one of the most important is the production costs associated with scale. Advertisers running native formats across many platforms require unique pieces of third-party publisher content to deliver a reader experience that's aligned with the publisher's editorial style. This would require bespoke brand content development for each platform.

While one-off, bespoke campaigns are more easily managed by marketers, it is the scale of this format that will deliver campaign reach. One solution that has been explored is buying publisher networks. In this case, there could potentially be the opportunity for advertisers to distribute the same creative across multiple sites without losing editorial context. While this is good in theory for larger markets, in smaller markets such as Australia the marketplace simply doesn't have the depth of networks to support this type of scaling.

Leveraging the channel

BuzzFeed's VP Motion Picture, Jonathan Perelman, uses the example of paid content distribution with the Toyota Prius. The case study demonstrates how storytelling using rich content shifted strongly held perceptions of the brand. While the environmental benefits of driving a hybrid car are high in people's minds, they are just not considered sexy or cool. Perelman maintains that for today's advertiser it's impossible to tell a brand's story in a banner ad.

Like most publishers, BuzzFeed offers brands paid brand/publisher native advertising. Perelman commented, 'Help tell a brand story in a different way, one that resonates with people'.[86]

Instead of using the Prius's selling proposition traditionally used in advertising, Toyota leveraged the high-ranking content formats and language found on the BuzzFeed platform to engage with its audience. 'The 20 Coolest Hybrid Animals' – face it, hybrids are just cooler, check out these awesome hybrid animals and get one of your own, like the Toyota Prius; or, 'The 20 Most Scenic Drives' – each drive featured in the top 20 is a long way from a petrol station, meaning the reader will need a hybrid vehicle. The Toyota case study demonstrates how to increase reach and effectiveness with paid content marketing used in the publisher's ecosystem.

Ways and means

General Electric (GE) is one of the world's oldest and largest company brands, stretching across the aviation, energy, finance and healthcare industries. GE's point of view on native advertising is simple: it doesn't matter who produces the content, as long as it's relevant, serves a need, and is in the right channel where it can be amplified. For example, to attract enthusiasts in specialty sectors, GE distributes images and videos of its products – from jet engines to

---

86   'Johnathan Perelman: Content is King, Distribution is Queen', Vimeo, 20 February 2014

wind turbines – using platforms such as Instagram and YouTube.

In partnership with BuzzFeed, GE promoted its sponsorship of the Paris Air Show. Using native content the brand and publisher worked collaboratively to create sponsored posts such as '16 Amazing Things That You'll See at an Air Show' and 'Incredible Flight Discoveries That You Didn't Know About'. Using gamification, BuzzFeed users could navigate and fly over a grid of GE articles using an aeroplane graphic. Interestingly, 'The people who influence and make large b-to-b purchases are the same people who enjoy consuming and sharing news and social emotional content on BuzzFeed.'[87]

Locally, GE has been partnering with the Australian media for over 12 months. The VP of Communications 'was initially sceptical readers would treat sponsored content the same as editorial.'[88] However, the brand discovered that their audience doesn't differentiate between brand/publisher developed content and the independent editorial. In partnership with *The Australian* newspaper, GE conducted a series of round-table discussions on Sky Business where their experts addressed challenges affecting businesses. The findings were then presented in editorial coverage on *The Australian* website and supported with weekly newsletters and co-branded advertising. 'The

---

87   Maura McGowan, 'GE Partners with BuzzFeed for B-to-B Native Ads', *Adweek*, 24 June 2013

88   Chris Byrne, 'Native Advertising Demystified Part 3: The Keys to Success', marketingmag.com.au, 6 March 2014

content reached over 1.7 million print readers, one million online readers, 76,000 Sky News viewers and received 9,507 video views.'[89]

Performance

What can't be ignored is that native content engagement rates are impressive. Felix Kruger, emerging solutions specialist at Fairfax Media, said that his firm's Brand Discover Platform had delivered engagement rates of over two minutes for native articles.[90] That compares to an average of around 30 seconds for advertorials and three to four minutes for editorial.

However, all too often marketers rely on publisher metrics such as engagement to analyse the effectiveness of native advertising: 'Native performance indicators such as visits, dwell rates and scroll depth are all good measures but they need be tied to user behaviour as this relates to marketing ROI.'[91] Ultimately brands need native ads to deliver on peer-to-peer sharing to measure a return on marketing investment, and this will require marketers to use tracking tags to identify the source.

---

89 Ibid

90 Brendan Coyne, 'Fairfax: Advertorial is dead, here's native 2.0', *AdNews*, 31 January 2014

91 Andrew Davies, 'Five Uncomfortable Truths About Native Advertising', Econsultancy, 6 May 2014

The rise of programmatic

Programmatic advertising is one of the hottest topics for advertisers globally, however many marketers still don't have a clear understanding of programmatic ad buying. If this is you then you're in the majority: '67% of marketers say they're unaware of automated media buying technology, don't understand it, or need to learn more about it to apply it to campaigns.'[92] This has come about from the overuse of industry jargon, acronyms, and interchangeable and inconsistent use of terminology. In fact, there are a number of methods to transact programmatic buying, which has further confused the understanding of the practice.

The term *programmatic* refers to the buying and selling of media inventory through real-time bidding (RTB) via automated auction services. Programmatic ad buying uses sophisticated, data-driven technology platforms and complex algorithms to buy the best performing ads for the advertiser's target audience with less wastage. At present, brands are predominantly using programmatic technology to plan and buy desktop, mobile and social advertising. However, what's set to change is data-driven automation of traditional offline media, with programmatic TV advertising poised to enter the media landscape.

---

92   Jack Marshall, 'Most Marketers Don't Understand Automated Ad Buying', CMO Today, *Wall Street Journal*, 31 March 2014

Data management technology

Data is providing marketers with unparalleled access to customer information such as location, language, times of interaction, purchase preferences and social interactions, which can be used to predict in real-time the needs and personal preferences of the user to deliver personalised brand experiences. Early adopter marketers with large data sets are capitalising on Data Management Platform (DMP) technology to combine first-party data (the brand's data) and third-party data to optimise ad targeting like never before.

In simple terms, a DMP is data warehousing. It is used to manage cookie IDs and audience segmentation to deliver deeper understanding of behaviour and optimise media and advertising. Marketers, agencies and publishers are embracing the platforms to collect and analyse data to create rich audience data sets. According to online publisher Digiday, 'in an attempt to take closer control of their data, some clients have begun licensing their own DMP technologies and managing those platform themselves.'[93] Marketers and agencies then use the data sets with demand side platforms (DSP) to plan their media buys.

Second screen syncing

The utilisation of multiscreen advertising is set to rapidly increase too, with second screen 'syncing' technology set

93   Jack Marshall, 'WTF is a Data Management Platform?', Digiday,
       15 January 2014

to once again shift how brands plan and buy their media. 'Second screen syncing is planning your media so that within seconds of your TV ad airing, a complementary ad appears on consumers' digital screens. Time-synced digital media plans use listening technology to identify when a specific TV ad airs; the technology then triggers the ad server to buy up available inventory across a network of sites, and the digital ad appears for a short period following the TV spot.'[94] With the technology, a brand could effectively serve an advertisement for a new model vehicle on TV and serve another ad, within seconds, to the viewer's smart device to book a test drive.

Cross-device advertising

Most marketers would be familiar with advertising retargeting. However, the big challenge for marketers is targeting their marketing messages to the same person across all their devices. Put simply, who is using which device in the household or workplace? There seems to be a great many providers offering cross-device targeting solutions, however compatibility across publishers, platforms and devices is still reliant on device identification methods.

Take a family household, for example: each member in the house has a smart phone, mum has an iPad and a desktop at work, the son has a personal laptop, and the

---

94   Digital & Media Predictions, Millward Brown, 2015

daughter has both a personal laptop and an iPad. Dad, he's a bit of a digital laggard with just his desktop at work.

Mum can't find her iPad so is researching holidays to New Zealand on her son's personal laptop, and a number of travel agencies are running marketing campaigns. The travel agents are using online advertising retargeting, where cookies (little pieces of data) are used to identify the user IP address on their website and then retarget their advertising messages on other websites they visit. When mum finishes her travel research she reads the news online and is served an ad for New Zealand. The son decides he wants his computer back to watch YouTube, and so for the next couple of days, guess who is being served ads for holidays to New Zealand? It is for this reason marketers should frequency cap their campaign, limiting the number of times the ad is seen on that device.

Retargeting ads to mobile audiences has its challenges too. Essentially, cookies are irrelevant on the mobile web, apps, TVs, wearables and cars. If a person is using a mobile device, is this same person using a desktop at work or a tablet at home, and at what part of the purchase journey are they using what device? This has led to an increasing demand from advertisers for a universal identifier tagging system.

The likes of Facebook, Google, YouTube and Amazon are creating personalised experiences for their audiences with a single platform login across all devices. So, no matter if the user is on mobile, desktop or tablet, the brand can serve its audience personalised communications or advertising.

Ad blocking

Blocking online ads on desktops has been around for a while now, however thanks to Google's efforts in removing ad blocking applications from its store, mobile ad blocking had been non-existent – that was, until Adblock Plus, one of the most popular ad blocking tools, launched its mobile browser. The Android browser automatically blocks mobile ads, claiming to save users up to '23% of a user's smartphone battery life, and also save on their data plan'.[95]

Marketing efforts in paid media – including native advertising, which has the same look and feel and editorial content on publishers' websites – can be blocked using the application, as will most ads appearing in social networking newsfeeds and display ads. Adblock Plus requires the ad networks such as Google to apply its 'acceptable ads list' before serving its ads; ads that don't make the list are typically pop-ups that interrupt the user experience. The larger entities – Google, Microsoft and Amazon – will pay hefty fees to have their ads served.

Ad blocking is on the rise. According to Business Insider Australia, 'the number of people with ad blockers installed worldwide grew 70% year to year to 144 million

---

95   Lara O'Reilly, 'One of the most popular ad blockers is releasing a mobile browser, which could be huge – but costly for companies like Google', Business Australia, 20 May 2015

in 2014'.[96] Should this trend continue unabated the free web as we know it could change forever, meaning the free content we've come to expect from publishers resides behind paywalls.

96   Lara O'Reilly, 'One of the most popular ad blockers is releasing a mobile browser, which could be huge – but costly for companies like Google', Business Australia, 20 May 2015

20

Sharing
the Buzz

Another key term on the lips of marketers is 'user-generated content'. Globally, agencies and brands are looking for ways to tap into the immense power of customer-to-customer generated content. It's how the Millennials – the next generation of customers who now represent a very large share of spending power in the economy and whose spending power will only increase as their earnings grow – are using non-traditional media to search, discover and explore brands. 'Unlike previous generations that consumed professionally-created content in magazines and on television, Millennials spend 30% of their media time on content created by their peers or the trusted sources they follow on social networks.'[97]

---

97   'Social Influence, Marketing's New Frontier', Ipso MediaCT, Research Paper, 2014

Peer generated content

User-generated content (UGC) is peer-to-peer or customer-to-customer created content and can include social media status updates, brand reviews, blogs, opinions and brand likes. Importantly, word-of-mouth marketing has become increasingly powerful in purchase decision-making. Coupled with the erosion of trust in brands and increasing scepticism of traditional marketing messages, word-of-mouth information Millennials receive is 'trusted 40% more than information they get from traditional media sources (TV, print & radio)'[98], meaning that in today's marketplace, UGC has become very influential and the most trusted source of information on brands for this generation of consumers.

Peer-generated content is vast, organic and influential, and also makes it difficult for marketers to control brand messaging. While the task for brands to rise above the noise of UGC is daunting, when marketers create programs with customer participation it inspires authentic content creation and encourages sharing. Authenticity is the result of content co-creation and a game changer for brands wanting to cut through the marketing noise. When brand experiences are relevant and have meaning in people's lives then participation is high. Coca-Cola's #ThisisAHH campaign – which encourages customers to create and share a 15-second video showing their 'Ahh moment' to

98 'Social Influence, Marketing's New Frontier', Ipso MediaCT,
    Research Paper, 2014

Instagram, Vine, Twitter, Facebook or Tumblr with the hashtag #ThisisAhh – is a recent example.

Coca-Cola's move from 'creative excellence to content excellence' was influenced by a shift in how and where their customers engaged with the brand. While their TV ads had been successful in shaping people's attitudes towards the brand, Coco-Cola's content strategy tapped into the idea of contagious brand stories that are weaved into popular culture, provide endless threads of highly relevant, sharable conversations. Storytelling is at the heart of our society; it's inherent in the way we communicate ideas, and how we educate and entertain, 'Consumers increasingly control marketing conversations, especially in the digital space. So it's up to marketers to make sure people want to talk about them...'[99]

Brands can influence and shape audience conversation around their brand's story, especially when the brand promise is weaved into the experience. Coco-Cola's 'Small World Machines' campaign built the brand's social purpose – to create significant positive change – into their storytelling using the idea of uniting India and Pakistan through 'new, open-hearted ways for people to come together, while highlighting the power of happiness.'[100] 'Coke created a warm and positive interaction between the users in the

99   Thomas Pardee, 'Coke's Wendy Clark at Digital Conference: Liquid and Links is Key', Ad Age, 6 April 2011

100   Shareen Pathak, 'Behind Coke's Attempt to Unite Indians & Pakistanis with Vending Machines', Ad Age, 20 May 2013

two countries.'[101] Using live streaming vending machines installed in two popular shopping centres, one in Lahore and the other in New Delhi, Coke asked their customers to put their differences aside and share a Coke with the intention of promoting cultural understanding.

Biggest buzz

Another UGC program built on higher purpose which won our hearts and minds was the 'Ice Bucket Challenge'. The challenge was started by baseball player Pete Frates, who was diagnosed with Amyotrophic Lateral Sclerosis (ALS) and challenged several Boston Red Sox players to the ice-bucket treatment to raise money for the condition. The first challenger was Frates, who nominated the players and challenged them to film themselves dumping a bucket of ice water on their heads. They then challenged one of their peers to do the same within 24 hours or donate to the cause.

The campaign went viral across Facebook, Twitter and Instagram, and within weeks Facebook newsfeeds were filled with challengers from the famous – Mark Zuckerburg, Oprah, Charlie Sheen and Steven Spielberg – to the everyday person wanting to participate, each dumping a bucket of iced water on their head and then nominating one of their friends. When Facebook released views and shares of the campaign, 'there had been more than 17 million videos

---

101   Shareen Pathak, 'Behind Coke's Attempt to Unite Indians & Pakistanis with Vending Machines', Ad Age, 20 May 2013

relating to the Ice Bucket Challenge shared and according to Facebook, these videos were viewed more than 10 billion times by more than 440 million people… From June 1 to Aug. 17, more than 28 million Facebook users talked about the Ice Bucket Challenge.'[102] The ALS Association reported $115 million raised and the organisation was introduced to millions of new donors.

Experiential

UGC is attracting attention from brands as a marketing lever for its ability to build participation in the experience by embedding the brand in the fabric of popular culture. Brands that have controlled their messaging are now relinquishing their tight grip and enabling customers to create their own brand experiences. My agency's work with condom manufacturer Ansell saw their brand SKYN embedded as an integral part of Schoolies Week in Australia, an event designed for school-leaving teens to celebrate finishing one chapter of their lives and beginning the next.

The SKYN brand promises users an 'intense feel', and for an audience unfamiliar with the category and the brand it was important to build brand affinity through contextual alignment. The brand promise was delivered through the customer discovery across social channels, outdoor, schoolies point-of-check-in, giant video screens at concerts, on-the-street sampling, and a 'take-over' built into an

---

102 Justin Lafferty, 'Updates Ice Bucket Challenge numbers: 17Million+ videos shared the Facebook', Social Times, 2014

activation using an extreme, bungie-styled ride to deliver an intense experience and shareable video, selfies, check-ins and posts with the brand in hand shared across users' social channels.

Peer-generated content programs are drivers of short-term buzz around the brand and have a place in the modern marketer's toolbox. Successful UGC campaigns create connections that empower fans to endorse the brand by enabling them to create brand stories using their own voice. However, creating sustainable networks of advocates who continue to advocate the brand requires more than a short-term campaign that engineers online conversations. Rather, it is the creation of great, everyday customer experiences that delivers advocacy – experiences that are relevant, simple, feel-good moments delivering the brand promise seamlessly at every customer/brand interaction; experiences which create an emotional connection that customers want to talk about.

21

Customer Surprise and Delight

The power of a customer feel-good moment can't be understated. When brands create unexpected moments that surprise and delight, this elicits positive emotional responses capable of shifting customer attitudes and providing experiences that people want to share with their social networks. These experiences can be as simple as empowering frontline customer service teams to solve problems real-time, using technology creatively to engage, and creating brand experiences that have the power to 'wow' and generate positive customer discussions.

A little love goes a long way

Facebook app company ShortStack sends thousands of subscriber emails and typically receives bounce-backs from members who are using their 'out of office' auto-respond. Their CEO and founder said, 'Most of the bouncebacks come from people who are on vacation. But sometimes there are messages like "I'm recovering from surgery" or

"I'm on maternity leave" or "I'm at a conference". We used to ignore these emails, but recently we started responding to some of them. We send along well wishes for the most part, but sometimes we share a link where the recipient can "order" a free company t-shirt. Of course we still get a few autoresponders for a second time, but we also get a heck of a lot of happy thank you notes when these folks return to work. We've also gotten a handful of really nice shout-outs on social media'.[103]

Welcome to our branch

The Commonwealth Bank in Australia has reinvented customer service and how they engage with their customers within their bricks and mortar branches. With a customer-centric approach to customer service, the bank focused on creating positive customer experiences through providing Branch Concierges. Typically, people who use physical banking services generally rate the banking experience as poor; the queues are long and there is never enough service staff. Commonwealth Bank has redesigned their branch experience so that from the moment a customer walks through the door they are engaged.

The Branch Concierge's role is to be knowledgeable on all aspects of the branch. They welcome, build rapport and guide customers to the right service provider who will fit their banking requirement. This superior level of customer

103   Jim Belosic, '3 Ways to Surprise and Delight Your Customers', Inc,
       2 March 2015

service delivers a unique and differentiated experience in comparison to other physical banking experiences in the Australian market. And, just as it was in 2013, the Commonwealth Bank was awarded the 2014 winner of the Roy Morgan Banking and Finance Satisfaction Awards, having won 11 of the year's monthly satisfaction awards.

Christmas wow!

For Christmas 2013, Canadian airline WestJet created a real-time Christmas Miracle for their customers because they wanted to show their customers that they cared. This was a very special experience that 'surprised and delighted', and put huge smiles on WestJet's customers' faces. It was a genuine and heartwarming idea that connected emotionally with passengers on the day, and with those of us who watched the YouTube video in the following weeks.

The experience journey started in the airline departure lounge, where customers could use the interactive large-screen monitors to scan their boarding passes and tell a live Santa their Christmas wish. The real-time giving was personalised from data on the boarding pass; Santa knew the travellers' names and their destinations. While travellers were en route to their destination, WestJest staff purchased, gift wrapped and gift tagged the presents customers had wished for. While travellers waited at the carousel for their luggage to arrive, snow began to fall, and instead of suitcases, Christmas presents began to appear, to smiles and tears all round. Just a wonderful customer experience moment.

Thirty-six million views on YouTube has made this customer 'surprise and delight' moment a viral hit, because the WestJet 'Christmas Miracle' created such a strong emotional connection. The WestJet experience demonstrated that the brand cared, and this random act of kindness initiated very positive online and offline word-of-mouth conversations about the brand. In today's experience economy, not only do customers want value and efficiency, they also need to feel good about doing business with a brand.[104]

While customer experience is more than a single interaction, this brand experience provided a memorable 'WestJet moment' that delivered their customers a 'surprise and delight' experience. Brands that connect emotionally with their customers by creating memorable moments in the brand/customer relationship help their customers to love doing business with them and provide opportunities that get people talking and recommending the brand.

104   Tom Springer, Domenico Azzarello & Jeff Melton, 'What It Takes to Win With Customer Experience', Bain & Company, 8 July 2011

22

Ready, Aim, Fire

It is impossible to predict how the world will look in the next five years. However, one thing is certain: the rapid pace of change driven by innovation will continue unabated. We are now super-connected and always-on, using our smart devices to connect anytime and anywhere, with expectations that our brand interactions will be personalised, contextual and device relevant. Technology will continue to fundamentally change how people interact with brands and customer expectations are set to increase further as the Internet of Things (IoT) creates tangible differences in people's lives, triggering more innovation, higher productivity, further economic growth and a new era of competition.

As drivers of change, marketers are perfectly placed to evolve their organisations' customer experiences, bringing together leadership and expertise in the areas of brand, customer, data, technology, innovation, marketing and digital design to positively influence internal alignment around customer relationships with brands. Brand leaders will need to shift their business focus from product to a whole-of-business, customer-centric approach encompassing people, processes and systems. Competitive advantage will be attributed to purpose-led organisations that meet their customers' needs by building customer-first cultures where the brand promise is consistently and seamless delivered across every touchpoint, turning satisfied customers into advocates.

The customer experience leader's toolbox will have to include measuring the customer/brand relationship – that is, the total customer experience – providing their organisation with actionable insights from different data sources to better understand the customer relationship, insights into purchasing behaviour, growth of customer recommendations, and future business performance. The toolbox will also be resourced to assist organisational alignment around the customer agenda – overcoming functional silos across marketing, customer service, sales, IT, HR and operations, and the processes and policies across the organisation aggregating a single focus behind delivering consistent, total customer experience.

For organisations operating in today's highly competitive and commoditised marketplace where customer relationships have traditionally been built on the back of transactional marketing practices, a brand's competitive advantage will be delivered from customer experiences that foster satisfaction and advocacy. In today's marketplace brand advocacy value represents market share growth, future revenues and profitability. While advocacy levels vary from category to category, research shows 'that the revenue growth of the brands with the highest advocacy levels is far above the industry average. Over time, that difference separates the leaders from the laggards.'[105]

As organisations' customer knowledge-base grows and marketers gain deeper insight into customer behaviour, brands will recognise the high importance of multi-layered experiences, giving their customers choices on how they interact with the brand. For this reason, brands will continue investment into building 'owned' channels, enabling them to produce relevant and real-time content for their audiences. With data-driven marketing the powerhouse behind contextual interactions, content will become highly personalised, adjusting to purchase lifecycle, place, time and device. From website search, automated email follow-ups, mobile app usage and social media, brands will pool data across multiple channels throughout the purchase journey to deliver experiences that provide customer value.

Now is the time where *Customer Experience is the Brand* and brand leaders are pivoting from communications experts to the custodians of total customer experience, creating relationships from the customer's perspective where customer needs are consistently met, brand promises are kept and great experiences are talked about and shared.

---

105 Pedro Esquivias, Steve Knox, Victor Sánchez-Rodríguez and Jody Visser, Boston Consulting Group, bcg perspectives, 'Fueling Growth Through Word of Mouth', 2 December 2013

About the author

Alex Allwood is a businesswoman and entrepreneur who believes that great experiences get people talking. For over 20 years she has helped brands grow by creating simple, feel-good customer experiences that people want to share with their peers and social networks.

Alex is the Founder and CEO of The Holla Agency, a media/creative firm that specialises in creating customer experiences combining data, insights, creative and strategy to connect brands and people in the right spaces, places and moments in time. The agency helps brands create emotional connections with customers using their Brand Strategy to Customer Experience Framework. The process defines brand purpose, reveals customer truths, aligns organisational culture around the customer to deliver and keep the brand promise, and creates great experiences that foster satisfaction and advocacy.

From leadership within her organisation to leadership within the marketing communications industry, Alex is a co-founder of The Communications Council Gender Diversity Group, a member of Rotary Club of Sydney Cove, and was awarded a Paul Harris Fellow in 2014 for her contribution to the ongoing work of Rotary. Alex is also a sought-after speaker and business mentor.

alexallwood.com.au

Bibliography

ADP Research Institute 2012, *Employee satisfaction vs. employee engagement: are they the same thing? An ADP white paper*.

ALS Association website, www.alsa.org.

Barnes, B 2013, 'At Disney parks, a bracelet meant to build loyalty (and sales)', *The New York Times*, 7 January.

Barton, C, Fromm J & Egan, C 2012, 'The Millennial consumer: debunking stereotypes', BCG Perspectives by The Boston Consulting Group.

Barton, C, Koslow, L & Beauchamp, C 2014, 'The reciprocity principle: how Millennials are changing the face of marketing forever', The Boston Consulting Group, January.

Belosic, J 2015, '3 ways to surprise and delight your customers', Inc.com, 2 March.

Beltran, F, Bhattacharjee, D, Fandel, H, Jones, B, Lippert, S & Ortega, F 2013, 'The secret to delighting customers? Put employees first', The Disney Institute blog, Disney Institute and McKinsey & Company, November.

van Bommel, E, Edelman, D & Ungerman, K 2014, 'Digitizing the consumer decision journey', McKinsey & Company Insights & Publications, June.

Botsman, R 2010, *The case for collaborative consumption*, TED Talk, TED.com.

Cameron, N 2015, 'How Flight Centre is mapping out a new kind of customer journey', CMO.com, 15 January.

—2015, 'Telstra's Inese Kingsmill shares how customer advocacy is elevating marketing's role', CMO.com, 17 February.

—2015, 'How NPS has helped NIB keep customers', CMO.com, 31 March.

—2015, 'How Telstra is applying data analytics to customer experience', CMO.com, 5 May.

Carlton, M 2013, *Co-creation in practice: how to innovate with the help of consumers*, event report, IPA Eff Fest, Warc, October.

Chipotle website, Investor Relations section.

CMO Council 2014, *Getting in sync with mobile customers*.

Coca-Cola, content strategy 2020.

Commonwealth Bank 2013, Sustainability reporting, www.commbank.com.au.

Contagious 2014, 'Privacy in perspective (and numbers)', Contagious.com, 12 May.

Costa, T 2014, 'Proactive experiences and the future of UX', *UX Magazine*, 2 April.

Coyne, B 2014, 'Fairfax: Advertorial is dead, here's native 2.0', *AdNews*, 31 January.

Crawford-Browne, S 2013, *Designing a branded customer experience*, GfK.

Cultivating Thought – Author Series website, www.cultivatingthought.com.

Davies, S 2014, 'Beyond the burrito: Chipotle's next big move', *Forbes*, 6 June.

Dawson, N 2014, 'Build trust in a post-privacy era', *Admap*, Warc, October.

Deloitte 2014, *Deloitte Mobile Consumer Survey 2014*.

Design for Experience Awards 2013, Award for Complete Customer Experience to Workshop Café.

—2014, Award for Complete Customer Experience to Workshop Café.

Donaldson, C 2014, 'CBA's 4 step plan: developing a customer centric mindset', *Inside HR*, 2 September.

Econsultancy & Adobe, *2015 Digital Trends Briefing*.

Edelman 2012, goodpurpose® study.

Esquivias, P, Knox, S, Sánchez-Rodríguez, S & Visser, J 2013, 'Fueling growth through word of mouth: introducing the brand advocacy index', *BCG Perspectives by the Boston Consulting Group*, 2 December.

Ferreira, H & Teixeira, AAC 2013, *'Welcome to the experience economy': assessing the influence of customer experience literature through bibliometric analysis*, working paper, FEP Economics and Management.

Fitzsimmons, C 2013, 'Inside Michelle Bridges' $67m body transformation empire', *BRW*, 9 July.

Foo, F 2014, 'Woolworths trials beacon specials in supermarket', *The Australian*, 11 November.

Goodman, J 2014, 'How to create a proactive customer experience', *Forbes*, 9 April.

The Guardian 2014, 'Mobile trends for 2015'.

Gustafsson, K 2014, 'Lego crowdsources its way to new toys', *Bloomberg Business*, 3 April.

Hower, M 2012, 'Run up to SB'12: an interview with Chris Arnold of Chipotle', *Sustainable Brands*, 28 May.

IAB Australia 2013, *Mobile Trends Report 2013*.

Ipsos MediaCT 2014, *Social influence, marketing's new frontier*, research paper.

Kalakota, R 2014, 'Guest personalization and wearable computing: Disney MyMagic+', Business Analytics 3.0.

Kapoor, R 2014, 'Lessons from the sharing economy', *TechCrunch*, 30 August.

Keller Fay Group 2013, 'What drives online vs. offline word of mouth: major differences revealed in new academic study'.

Kennedy, J 2013, 'Brands as publishers', in an interview of Matt Pinkney (head of content at AFL Media) for 'The Brief – content marketing and AFL Media', *B&T Magazine*.

Krigsman, M 2014, 'Bridging the gap between brand promise and customer experience', ZDNet, 1 June.

Lafferty, J 2014, 'Updated Ice Bucket Challenge numbers: 17M+ videos shared to Facebook', *SocialTimes*.

Leggett, K 2014, 'Forrester's top trends for customer service in 2014', Forrester.com, 13 January.

Manning, H & Bodine, K 2012, *Outside in, the power of putting customers at the center of your business*, Forrester Research.

Marketo 2014, *Improve customer acquisition with an engagement strategy*, Marketo.com.

Marquis, C & Park, A 2014, 'Inside the buy-one give-one model', *Stanford Social Innovation Review*.

Marriott Travel Brilliantly website, Marriott Hotels.

Marshall, J 2014, 'Most marketers don't understand automated ad buying', *The Wall Street Journal*, 31 March.

—2014, 'WTF is a data management platform?', *Digiday*.

Mathieu, M 2014, speech at AANA Global Marketer Conference.

McCrindle Pty Ltd 2014, *Australia's Generational Profile*, 20 February.

McGowan, M 2013, 'GE partners with BuzzFeed for B-to-B native ads', *Adweek*.

Millward Brown 2014, *Brandz™ Top 100 Most Valuable Global Brands 2014*.

—2015, *2015 Digital & Media Predictions*.

—Brand Ideal, the study.

Mishra, R, 'The game-changing nature of beacons', *UX Magazine*.

MSLGROUP & PR Week slideshare 2014, 'Brand purpose, Millennials and the epic creative that engages them'.

Net Promoter Community, 'The Net Promoter score and system', www.netpromoter.com.

News.com.au 2014, 'Is Uber really worth $48 billion?', *Money* section, 8 December.

Nielsen 2013, 'Global trust in advertising and brand messages', Nielsen.com, 17 September.

—2014, 'Millennials: breaking the myths', Nielsen.com.

Norman, A 2012, 'The Wal-Mart/Facebook social genome', *The Huffington Post*.

Nysveen, H & Pedersen, P 2014, 'Influences of co-creation on brand experience: the role of brand engagement', *International Journal of Market Research*, vol. 56, no. 6, pp. 807–832.

O'Reilly, L 2015, 'One of the most popular ad blockers is releasing a mobile browser, which could be huge – but costly for companies like Google', *Business Insider Australia*.

Oracle 2011, *2011 Customer Experience Impact Report: Getting to the heart of the consumer and brand relationship*.

Oremus, W 2014, 'Facebook's privacy pivot', *Slate Magazine*.

Owyang, J 2014, 'Disruption from the collaborative economy', www.webstrategist.com.

Pardee, T 2011, 'Coke's Wendy Clark at digital conference: liquid and links is key', *Advertising Age*, 6 April.

Pathak, S 2013, 'Behind Coke's attempt to unite Indians and Pakistanis with vending machines', *Advertising Age*, 20 May.

—2014, 'Fitting room 2.0: a three-screen experience to help you try on jeans', *Digiday*.

Perelman, J 2014, 'Content is king, distribution is queen', Vimeo.

Pine II, BJ & Gilmore, JH 1998, 'Welcome to the experience economy', *Harvard Business Review*, July.

Procter & Gamble, Connect + Develop program website.

Pulido, A, Stone, D & Strevel, J 2014, 'The three Cs of customer satisfaction: consistency, consistency, consistency', McKinsey & Company Insights & Publications.

Rawson, A, Duncan, E & Jones, C 2013, 'The truth about customer experience', *Harvard Business Review*.

Rich Women List for 2015, *BRW*.

Riedy, C 2013, 'The sharing economy spooking big business', *The Conversation*.

Roy Morgan Banking and Finance Satisfaction Awards 2014.

Same, S & Larimo, J 2012, 'Marketing theory: experience marketing and experiential marketing'.

Schmidt-Subramanian, M 2014, 'The state of voice of the customer programs, 2014: it's time to act', Forrester.

Schmitt, B 2011, 'Experience marketing: concepts, frameworks and consumer insights', *Foundations and Trends® in Marketing*, 18 May.

Schneider, M 2015, 'Designing for place at the Home Depot', *UX Magazine*.

Share a Coke campaign post-analysis, marketing.com.au, 2012.

Sinek, S 2009, *How great leaders inspire action*, TED Talk, TED.com.

Springer, T, Azzarello, D & Melton, J 2011, 'What it takes to win with customer experience', Bain & Company, 8 July.

Stengel, J 2014, *Grow: how ideals power growth and profit at the world's greatest companies*.

Temkin Group 2014, 'The ultimate customer experience infographic, 2014', *Customer Experience Matters*.

Tinlin, L 2014, 'In pursuit of brand purpose', *Market Leader*, Warc.

Unilever Dove website.

UX Magazine staff 2014, 'Announcing winners in the international Design for Experience Awards,' *UX Magazine*, 21 March.

Warc 2012, 'Warc Briefing: Co-creation'.

Whiteside, S 2013, *Five crucial B2B marketing lessons from General Electric*, event reports, ANA Masters of Marketing, Warc, October.

Wikipedia entry, customer lifetime value.

—disruptive innovation.

—Toyota Prius.

World Federation of Advertisers (WFA) & Firefly Millward Brown 2011, Project Reconnect.

Yamnitsky, M 2013, 'Three proactive assistance startups worth watching', *Forrester*.

Yu, F 2014, *Bridging the digital divide: how CMOs can rise to meet 5 expanding expectations*, Deloitte Development LLC.

Zambito, T 2014, 'The CMP modern marketing guide to buyer personas and buyer insights research (part 3)', *Customer Think*.